Through The Eyes of a Canine

How changing your perception and understanding the emotional life of your dog can create a stable and Harmonious pack

By David J. Kurlander

Through the Eyes of a Canine

How changing your perseption and understanding the

emotional life of your dog

can create a stable and harmonious pack

To request permission, contact the publisher at

David@ThePackAnimalPodcast.com

Paperback: ISBN 978-1-7372187-1-5

Hardcover: ISBN 978-1-7372187-0-8

Ebook: ISBN 978-1-7372187-2-2

Library of Congress Control Number: 2021920389

Author: David J. Kurlander

Illustrator: Shaun L. Smith

To purchase this book in bulk for promotional, educations, or

business use,

or to request in-person appearances, please contact us at:

Winds Of Fate Publishing, LLC

Deer Lodge, Tennessee, United States Of America

David@ThePackAnimalPodcast.com

It does not matter how much time you spend with the wolf; it is within the capacity of your mind to open and become the wolf.

—David J. Kurlander

I dedicate this book, my heart and soul, and all that it manifests,
to my two boys

Brogan & Bjørn.

ACKNOWLEDGEMENTS

A special thanks to all the families, past and present, for allowing

me the opportunity to be a part of you and your dog's life. Each

and every experience with you and your dogs has taught me

something new, not only about the way canines perceive the

world, but how we influence the world as humans, and how we

can make positive changes to reconnect with that which is most

important. The process of learning is infinite, especially with the

ever-changing dynamics of life. Stay strong and remember that

your dogs need you, especially in the most challenging of times.

To the countless canines, both wild and domestic, thank you for

accepting me as part of your pack. There may have been a time in

your life when all seemed to be lost within a dark cloud of

confusion, yet you pulled through that darkness to shine even

brighter than the sun. You have taught me that love has no

bounds along with the power to crumble the thickest walls. Your courage to let go of the past and open your hearts with unconditional love should serve as a lesson to all. You inspire me and are the heart and soul of this multi-layered literary journey. You are my most profound teachers and the heroes within the pages of my personal story.

My deepest thanks to Melissa Leo and Barbara Landau. Words cannot fully express the depth of my gratitude. Your immense generosity has helped me to manifest such a monumental dream. You have opened a whole new world of possibilities for the Kurlander pack, both two-legged and four. Most importantly, I am grateful for your devout friendship and unwavering belief in me and this book.

My heartfelt appreciation goes to Jenn Brown, writer and editor, for walking with me through this literary journey and bringing my ideas into written fruition. Your writing finesse and editing brought about the best version of this book.

Thank you to Stephanie Carroll, copy editor, for your keen eye and help with polishing this manuscript.

Many thanks to Shaun L. Smith (illustrator) and Matthew Savoury (graphic arts and cover designer) for your immense artistic talent, which has greatly enriched the content of this book.

A special thank you to Dr. Christos Suriano for writing such an insightful forward. Your words and knowledge have contributed to the depth of content and helped to usher forward the pages within this book. I have nothing but the highest respect and admiration for you, my friend.

Thank you to my sister, Virginia Murphy, for critiquing various parts of this manuscript, and for your expert notes and final editing touches.

To my parents, James and Rosemary Kurlander, thank you for encouraging my love for animals from the very beginning of my life and never suppressing who I was always destined to become. To my wife, Tammy Kurlander, your love, support, and guidance has helped me to realize my true inner potential. You believed in me during the most challenging of times and lifted my head when I lost faith in myself. Words cannot express how grateful I am to have found you.

Finally, a deeply heartfelt thank you to all my family and friends, both near and far, and my mentors for your continued support and encouragement. You are the essence of hope and a breath of life on this planet.

Table of Contents

Contents, Continued

Foreword

By Dr. Christos Suriano

It is natural for us to anthropomorphize, or attribute human characteristics to, other animals. As a scientist, I will even anthropomorphize the proteins and genes that I study in the laboratory, assuming that they willingly perform functions and move around cells with intent. But in order to fully appreciate the biology of the domesticated animals that we interact with on a daily basis, including our dogs, we must understand the unique set of sensory experiences, perceptions, and cognitive abilities that they possess or utilize as they, in turn, try to understand us.

Every species of animal experience the world around them in a unique way. As humans, with our limited set of sensory apparatuses and neural accoutrement, we will likely never experience the world as many animals do. However, by understanding how their brains function and by observing how they behave, we can begin to approximate how some animals perceive and interact with their world. Aquatic animals are a great example of how sensory experiences can differ between species due to the medium of their environment.

Sharks and their relatives, termed elasmobranchs, have evolved a wonderfully sensitive electrosense that they use to detect potential prey, conspecifics, and the magnetic fields of the Earth[1]. From heartbeats and muscle contractions to nerve conduction, animals give off bioelectric signals that conduct relatively well in seawater. Using specialized electroreceptors and neural circuits, sharks and other elasmobranchs can sense these bioelectric signals at close range and use it to locate their prey.

On the other hand, some animals have lost sensory systems that no longer provide adaptive value in new environments. For example, some fish species living in the Lower Congo River have reduced eyesight, or lost eye functionality altogether, as a result of living in conditions with high turbidity and low visibility. However, they compensate for this loss by increasing the importance of other sensory systems that better serves the fish in these conditions[2–4]. Some of these fish have also evolved the ability to purposefully give off bioelectric signals using specialized muscles and nerves, termed electric organs[5], which they use to communicate with conspecifics (and in some cases hunt[6] or provide self-defense[7]). Take a moment to imagine living in an aquatic environment, having no functional eyesight, being incredibly sensitive to the movement of water over your skin, and using electrical signals to "feel" the world around you. It is quite a different existence than our own and seems almost alien.

Of course, the examples I've written about here concern the special lives of fish because their lives stand in such sharp contrast to our own. But birds and mammals have evolved novel sensory systems to interact with their world as well. Some birds can see greater portions of the electromagnetic spectrum; in addition to "visible light" (so called because we use this portion of the spectrum), some birds extend their visible range into ultraviolet wavelengths and thus see new forms of color[8,9]. Think about what it would be like to use echolocation, which is used by some bats[10] and dolphins[11]. Amazingly, platypuses have independently evolved their own form of electroreception[12]. This list is by no means comprehensive, but merely points out the myriad ways that animals are uniquely able to sense and interact with their environment. Animals of all sorts, including our dogs, experience the world in ways that are different than us and we should keep this in mind as we interact with them.

We are generally well aware of a dog's sensitive hearing (auditory) and/or smelling (olfactory) capabilities. Dogs can use these sensory systems to provide services to humans, including the detection of explosives, drug compounds, hazardous materials, and even individuals infected with a virus[13–15]. But these service dogs are few in number compared to canines kept purely for companionship.

Due to our close co-habitation, we generally understand dog vocalizations and basic body language quite well from a young age. But less well known is how dogs have evolved to understand *our* emotions, mannerisms, and body language. For example, when talking to one another, humans will often look at the right eye of the person that they are conversing with. It is thought that this side of the face is more expressive than the left side, allowing us to better judge the other person's emotional state. This phenomenon is called left gaze bias. Amazingly, dogs have evolved to perform this left gaze bias when looking at humans, but not when looking at the faces of monkeys or other dogs, indicating some species specificity to this behavior[16]. Correspondingly, dogs can differentiate smiling from neutral faces[17] as well as a range of other emotional states from their owner. In addition to the visual detection of emotion, dogs may also be able to detect our emotional states by smelling olfactory cues that we release[18]. Just as dogs display some asymmetry when they view a person's face, they may also use different nostrils to detect human vs. canine odors during stressful situations[19]. From sensation to cognition, dogs can follow a human's point to retrieve an object, far outperforming chimpanzees at this task[20].

After all that dogs have evolved to do for us, the least we can do is reciprocate this attempt at understanding. By anthropomorphizing canines, we are ignoring their entire natural history, the evolutionary pressures that have forged their unique sensory systems, their cognitive capabilities, and most importantly, what makes them such great partners for humankind.

I have had the pleasure of being friends with David for many years. There are few people more qualified to understand the unique ways that canines perceive and react to their specific world. Almost every conversation that David and I have touches on the different types of animals that he has worked with, either at the Bronx Zoo or beyond, and how every species of animal is special. By understanding dogs in this way, hopefully we may realize that behaviors that we have labeled as "troublesome", may in fact be natural to our dogs. They are only labeled as "troublesome" because of our inter-species co-habitation. In this book, David teaches us how to address these behaviors and to see the world from the dog's point of view, a task that I have hopefully shown is no small task. Ultimately, by understanding the world through a canine's eyes, we can become better companions to our canine friends and understand each other more deeply.

Sincerely,

Christos Suriano, PhD

References

1. Newton, K. C., Gill, A. B. & Kajiura, S. M. Electroreception in marine fishes: chondrichthyans. *J. Fish Biol.* **95**, 135–154 (2019).

2. Schobert, C. S. *et al.* Comparative ocular anatomy in a blind African cichlid fish, Lamprologus lethops. *Vet. Ophthalmol.* **16**, 359–364 (2013).

3. Alter, S. E., Brown, B. & Stiassny, M. L. J. Molecular phylogenetics reveals convergent evolution in lower Congo River spiny eels. *BMC Evol. Biol.* **15**, 224 (2015).

4. Soares, D. & Niemiller, M. L. Sensory Adaptations of Fishes to Subterranean Environments. *BioScience* **63**, 274–283 (2013).

5. Bell, C. C., Zakon, H. & Finger, T. E. Mormyromast electroreceptor organs and their afferent fibers in mormyrid fish: I. Morphology. *J. Comp. Neurol.* **286**, 391–407 (1989).

6. Catania, K. The shocking predatory strike of the electric eel. *Science* **346**, 1231 (2014).

7. Catania, K. C. Power Transfer to a Human during an Electric Eel's Shocking Leap. *Curr. Biol.* **27**, 2887-2891.e2 (2017).

8. Goldsmith, T. H. What Birds See. *Sci. Am.* **295**, 68–75 (2006).

9. Rajchard, J. Ultraviolet (UV) light perception by birds: a review. *Veterinární Medicína* **54**, 351–359 (2009).

10. Jones, G. & Teeling, E. C. The evolution of echolocation in bats. *Trends Ecol. Evol.* **21**, 149–156 (2006).

11. Harley, H. E., Putman, E. A. & Roitblat, H. L. Bottlenose dolphins perceive object features through echolocation. *Nature* **424**, 667–669 (2003).

12. Pettigrew, J. D. Electroreception in monotremes. *J. Exp. Biol.* **202**, 1447–1454 (1999).

13. Furton, K. G. & Myers, L. J. The scientific foundation and efficacy of the use of canines as chemical detectors for explosives1Invited paper for the special issue of Talanta 'Methods for Explosive Analysis and Detection'.1. *Talanta* **54**, 487–500 (2001).

14. Beebe, S. C., Howell, T. J. & Bennett, P. C. Using Scent Detection Dogs in Conservation Settings: A Review of

Scientific Literature Regarding Their Selection. *Front. Vet. Sci.* **3**, 96 (2016).

15. Essler, J. L. *et al.* Discrimination of SARS-CoV-2 infected patient samples by detection dogs: A proof of concept study. *PLOS ONE* **16**, e0250158 (2021).

16. Guo, K., Meints, K., Hall, C., Hall, S. & Mills, D. Left gaze bias in humans, rhesus monkeys and domestic dogs. *Anim. Cogn.* **12**, 409–418 (2009).

17. Nagasawa, M., Murai, K., Mogi, K. & Kikusui, T. Dogs can discriminate human smiling faces from blank expressions. *Anim. Cogn.* **14**, 525–533 (2011).

18. D'Aniello, B., Semin, G. R., Alterisio, A., Aria, M. & Scandurra, A. Interspecies transmission of emotional information via chemosignals: from humans to dogs (Canis lupus familiaris). *Anim. Cogn.* **21**, 67–78 (2018).

19. Siniscalchi, M., d'Ingeo, S. & Quaranta, A. The dog nose "KNOWS" fear: Asymmetric nostril use during sniffing at canine and human emotional stimuli. *Behav. Brain Res.* **304**, 34–41 (2016).

20.   Kirchhofer, K. C., Zimmermann, F., Kaminski, J. &

Tomasello, M. Dogs (Canis familiaris), but Not Chimpanzees

(Pan troglodytes), Understand Imperative Pointing. *PLOS*

ONE **7**, e30913 (2012).

I do not wish to be seen as an authority. Rather, I wish to serve as a voice for those animal beings who cannot speak our language and as a guide for open-minded humans who wish to begin the journey of developing a thoughtful and satisfying interspecies relationship.

—David J. Kurlander

Introduction

It was a beautiful spring morning, the kind where a seven-year-old kid who loves climbing trees would trade his favorite comic book not to be sitting in a classroom in Santa Maria Elementary School on Zerega Avenue in the Bronx. But there I was.

One of the sisters opened the window to let in some fresh air and said good morning as she did every day, oblivious to my longing to be outdoors with the rest of the living world. As she spoke, a squirrel that I had been watching in the tree outside cautiously approached the open window. He sniffed the air, and with one bounding leap jumped onto the teacher's desk, following his keen sense of smell to the bowl of assorted nuts that the nuns kept nearby to snack on throughout the day. Grabbing one, he quickly absconded with it out the window and back into the tree, where he sat, tail curled along his spine, and enjoyed his pilfered snack.

I was astonished! This small event, which probably lasted no more than 45 seconds, was a pivotal moment in my life. I dwelled on it for months. Each morning that summer, I would rise with the sun and hastily get dressed. Not lingering over breakfast, I would grab my plastic binoculars and hurry outside to spend time with my animal friends.

I spent days gazing into the green canopy of swaying leaves, imagining how it would feel to be a squirrel or a bird, hopping from branch to branch with such ease. What did they do with their days? Did they notice me sitting there watching them? What were they thinking? Could they even think at all? What was it like to be them?

If it was a rainy day, I spent hours in our barn. We lived in one of the original homes built in the Bronx before it became part of New York City, and were lucky to have a small yard and even a small barn. I would sit in a musty corner, get as still as I could manage, and wait. The barn would eventually come to life with brown and gray mice scurrying around, foraging for food, and communicating with each other in some undetectable way. I imagined them returning home with their scavenged harvest to serve up a great feast for their families.

MY FIRST CANINE COMPANION

And there was my husky Brandy—my best friend. I spent my days with him, and if my mother could not find me, she knew to look for me snuggled up with Brandy in the dog house out back. Not only was he my companion, he was also my protector. Once he buckled the chain link fence around our yard when I came running home after a strange man approached me while I was playing down the street. As I reached the driveway and shouted for Brandy—in abject fear as this man pursued me—my canine companion shot out of his house like lightning, ready to protect and defend.

When I was with Brandy, I felt safe, like nothing was wrong in the world and like no one could touch me. Later, I would come to understand that this is what it means to be part of a pack. It was love in its purest form and the foundation of my later understanding of the deep bond between humans and canines.

Throughout all this, my parents supported my love of animals and my preference to spend time with the non-human world. They gave me parakeets and lizards as pets. They never complained when I took in insects, raised them, and released them. And they understood that I preferred to spend time with Brandy more than I did with most people, except for my best friend, Rob Moran, who was part of our pack. My folks understood that I generally preferred the company of animals to humans.

CITY MOUSE TO COUNTRY MOUSE

While I squeezed as much nature as I could out of my childhood neighborhood in the Bronx, I was excited when my parents decided to relocate to upstate New York, about an hour north of the city. Exchanging sky scraping apartment buildings and polluted air for the whispering silence of towering trees and crisp breezes dramatically changed my life.

As did high school.

Being a loner who prefers to spend his time with animals may have been a perk for my parents who did not have to entertain me, but it did not bode well for high school, where my chances of survival were worse than a lone gazelle beset by a pride of lions.

To escape the incessant bullying I encountered at lunch, I would find other things to do with myself, like spending time with Mr.

Beaman, the animal behavior and field biology teacher, cleaning the classroom and caring for the school's small collection of animals. He was a massive influence and inspiration in my life. He modeled what it meant to be kind and compassionate toward our animal brothers and sisters and the environment as a whole.

Once he caught a bumblebee and brought it over to me. He placed the bee in my hand and offered me a powerful lesson about how appearances can be deceiving. He explained that while most people see bees at best as a nuisance and at worst as harmful and dangerous if we look past our initial perception, we discover they have a beautifully complex social structure and play an important role in our ability to have such a bountiful produce section in the grocery store. He taught me to look deeper and realize that animals' lives are precious, just like ours, and that all life deserves respect and consideration.

ON THE SCENT OF MY TRUE PATH

At a young age, I got my first job at a small mom-and-pop pet store cleaning cages and tanks. All the money I earned went right back into the store to "rescue" the animals I was taking care of. I had one goal: work hard and use my money to save animals. Gratefully, my parents tolerated the never-ending parade of creatures that I brought home.

In this job, I met a customer who was a reptile breeder and inventor of several products used by zoos and herpetologists. I was fascinated by amphibians and reptiles and whenever he would visit the store, I would pick his brain about rare species, particularly why some of them were so hard to breed. My theory was that our sterile cages were too unnatural for them. I wondered if they needed an environment more similar to their wild homes where light, temperature, and moisture reflected what their biology was accustomed to after so many thousands of years.

On one particular visit, I watched this customer set up and demonstrate a super-fine misting system for tanks. I immediately wondered how this could be used to simulate the natural conditions in which a reptile would have lived. Curious, I decided to experiment. I collected some PVC pipe, wire, ceramic light sockets, silicone tubing, sprinkler timers, and some of his micro misting nozzles and created a large, arched structure that could be mounted over a tank. It included light bulbs of different intensities—spanning from daylight to moonlight, harnessing UVA and UVB rays—each one with a fader and a timer. The misting system was set up on separate timers and, depending on the animal, was positioned to rain directly overhead or to spray in opposing directions at various times to simulate monsoonal weather.

As luck would have it, I was able to successfully breed some very difficult to propagate reptiles and amphibians. I gained some recognition in herpetology circles, which was quite exciting for an awkward, geeky teenager—though as you can imagine, this did nothing for my social standing among my peers.

BEHIND THE GLASS

Eventually, I was invited to assist with the installation of a misting system at the Bronx Zoo as a volunteer. I jumped at the opportunity. It was a dream come true to step from the spectator side of the thick glass, where I had been an observer all my life, to the steamy tropical rainforest on the other side. Soon after, I became a volunteer for the Department of Herpetology where I worked with the reptile and amphibian collection. Over time, I managed to introduce myself to every keeper, manager, and curator at the zoo until I was offered a full-time position in the Department of Ornithology. While I loved amphibians, reptiles, and birds, I was eager to work with the mammals and quickly transferred to that department when another position opened up.

During my tenure at the zoo, I was trained by the Wildlife Conservation Society to be a Wild Animal Keeper. Continuing with my interest in understanding how animals lived in their natural environments and how that translated into their lives with us, I specialized in behavior and captive wild animal enrichment. I thought a lot about how to make an animal's life at the zoo feel as close to their life in the wild as possible. I knew it would never be the same, but it could always be closer to what they knew biologically, and I thought we owed them that.

I worked with every animal at the zoo, but none captured my attention and imagination more than the wolves. I became obsessed. I would spend most of my free time observing wolves at sanctuaries throughout the region. The rest of my time I spent digging into the zoo's documents and research. I thought if I compared the behaviors and activities of wolves in the wild with their behaviors and interactions in captivity, I could help create a more natural environment to satisfy our captive population.

But once I had the opportunity to observe wolves in the wild, I started questioning some of the conclusions of the research I had been studying. I discovered holes in the data that were explained away by ideas and beliefs that were clearly human-centric and did not jive with what I observed in wild or captive wolves. It seemed to me that the animal's point of view was rarely considered, and I began to realize there was more than one way to study and interact with animals.

My approach, from that initial encounter with the squirrel in the classroom at Santa Maria School, had instinctively been to always think from the animal's point of view. That is, to get inside their minds and use our capacity for imagination and perspective-taking to experience the world with their senses. As I worked with the wolves, I realized that I learned the most about another species when I suspended my own way of seeing and shifted my perspective to see through their eyes. This not only opened up my experience with the wolves, but it also paved the way for a new understanding of—and a new way of working with—our domestic canines.

BREAKING FROM THE PACK

What I do does not easily fall into a category like *dog trainer, dog psychologist, animal behaviorist,* or *researcher*—although my work contains elements from each of those approaches. Taken alone, each of these fields fell short for me in some way as I continued to work professionally with animals. Do not get me wrong— there are good people doing good work and getting results in all of those fields. But each time I opened an animal behavior textbook, read a research paper, or saw a dog trainer use unnecessary force or unnatural methods to get a dog to perform unnatural tasks (like "sit," "stay," or "come"), I instinctively felt it was disconnected from the reality of what I experienced with the animals themselves.

Much like I have done in my life since childhood, I continue to follow my instincts and investigate on my own. I study the work of the giants of science who came before us, like Charles Darwin, and Konrad Lorenz, the founder of ethology (the study of animal behavior). I learn much from the research of people like geneticist Dmitry Belyayev, whose fox breeding experiments gave us incredible insights into canine behavior and the process of domestication. I engage in regular conversation with scientists like naturalist, archaeoastronomer, and author Bernie Taylor and Princeton neuroscientist Dr. Christos Suriano. And then I hold everything up against my own experience.

Along the way, I have been deeply inspired by Dr. Jane Goodall. Best known for her work with chimpanzees, Dr. Goodall is a tireless advocate for all species who helped me understand and articulate the deeper connections that are possible between dogs and people. "We're not the only beings on the planet with personalities, minds, and feelings. That gives us a new respect, not only for the chimpanzees, but the other amazing animal beings with whom we share the planet," she said in a 2006 talk. In a conversation with National Public Radio in 2020, she perfectly articulated the opportunity we have with our furry family members to shift our perspective toward one that honors all life. "When I was a child, I had this wonderful teacher, and that was my dog, Rusty. And he taught me that in this respect, the professors were absolutely wrong: We are not the only beings on the planet with personality, mind, and emotion," she explained.

I find her philosophy is in-line with my own observations, that while we are asking dogs to become part of our human lives, we cannot treat them like they are humans. They have their own unique way of seeing the world, and our goal should be a relationship of mutuality, not one of master and servant.

Seeing animals as autonomous beings with their own points of view and ways of experiencing the world is natural to me. Squirrels, mice, ants, lizards, birds, wolves—I have been putting myself in their place for as long as I can remember, sensing the world through their eyes and modifying my relationship to them as a result. My success with resolving behavior issues with dogs is a testament to this capacity.

Understanding the natural structure and communication of the canine world, combined with the ability to see the world through their eyes, allows me to understand a dog's needs and enables me to relay this information to "their person." I do not see myself as a ruler or an authority; I see myself as a liaison or translator for dogs who are speaking loudly but are not being understood by most people.

I am keenly aware that most people do not relate to their dogs in this way. When people call someone like me, they usually just want to "fix bad behavior," often as quickly as possible. They need their dog to stop or start doing something (like stop chewing on everything and start coming when called), but they do not consider the situation from the dog's point of view.

My work is to help people understand that the problem will not be solved just by "fixing the dog," because that is not where the issue is. What will make a difference is learning to relate to their dog in an open-minded and thoughtful way. Relationship is everything, and the beauty and complexity of the relationship between dogs and humans is unlike any other interspecies partnership. Once there is a basic understanding of a dog's need for structure, safety, and crystal-clear communication, you have a foundation on which to work with any behavior problems or successfully train your companion for hunting, agility, or other pursuits.

LEARNING TO THINK LIKE YOUR DOG

For more than two decades, I have honed my theories and tested them against real-life work with more than 150,000 dogs and their human companions. This book is a distillation of what I have learned so far. It provides suggestions for how to deal with biting, chewing, growling, and more (see Chapter 7)—but, more importantly, it offers you a new way to think of your relationship with your best friend. It gives you the tools you need to shift your perception so you can create a mutually satisfying life with your four-legged family members. So, while you could skip ahead to the chapter on solving common behavior problems, you may not find my suggestions all that helpful if you have not spent the time learning how to see the world through your dog's eyes by reading the previous chapters.

In Chapter 1, we will venture into the past to see what we know about the start of the human/canine relationship, which is arguably the most important interspecies relationship in human history. While the origin of our alliance is still shrouded in mystery, we explore what we have learned from the last few hundred years of domestic breeding, and we look at what a relationship of mutuality looks like.

A relationship of mutuality does not require that we anthropomorphize our canine companions. In fact, anthropomorphism—treating dogs as if they are humans—is one of the biggest consequences of our misunderstanding of the nature of the human/canine relationship. It causes us to dress up our dogs as children and to project our human psychology onto them—but they are not human, and our psychological concepts do not apply in that context.

In Chapter 2, we look at the fallacy of anthropomorphism and discover how to begin to shift our perception through an exploration of quantum theory. We explore a different perspective on consciousness, which can give us a new way of seeing and being.

In Chapter 3, we will also explore how your attitude is the key to success with your dog. Without exaggeration, 90% of the problems I see are problems with the relationship between a person and their dog. This is good news because when one side of a relationship changes, the other side must shift, too. It is our responsibility, as providers for our canine companions, to take the initiative to fix that relationship.

If you feel lost, defeated, confused, angry, or any other negative emotion about your dog, it will affect your relationship with them in the same way it affects your human relationships. You have the power to fix almost any problematic situation you encounter by embracing failure, seeing something from a different perspective, pulling from the infinite options in the field of potentiality, and trying something new. Luckily, these skills are trainable through practices like mindfulness, reframing, perspective-taking, and developing curiosity. As you practice these skills, you create an environment that will help your dog thrive and will probably improve your relationship with the humans in your life as well.

As you learn to attune to the unseen and adjust your perception to sense that which is beyond the obvious, you open the door to knowing dogs on their own terms and to recognizing them for their unique characteristics, many of which are associated with their particular breed. In Chapter 3, we discuss personality and genetic predisposition among breeds, and how understanding a dog's inherent purpose can help you understand their needs and fulfill those needs by giving them an appropriate task. When they are living out their soul-driven purpose and are able to contribute to the health and safety of the pack, they live a happier life and are much less likely to act in ways we view as problematic. In this chapter, we will also touch on which breed might be a good fit for you given your lifestyle.

In Chapter 4, we look at two crucial elements to understanding how your dog sees the world: structure and communication. Dogs are pack animals and literally need a pack to survive. We look at some of the common misconceptions about pack life and explore how to translate the rules and social norms of a wild pack into a human/canine pack. And we focus on communication, taking cues from how mamma wolves work with their young, and learn about the three necessary components for good communication: emotion, compromise, and effort.

Once we understand how to shift our perspective and look for our dog's inherent tendencies and individual personality—and once we have a grasp on structure and communication—we can then take the leap into behavior and training in Chapters 5 and 6. Working with a dog's behavior is not the same thing as training a dog. We will explore the differences and discuss detailed approaches for each. I will also weigh in on devices (e.g., electric collars and fences), as well as various training techniques (e.g., what I call the "vending machine methods" and the "do it or I will hurt you" methods). These chapters are where you will really start to see my philosophy in action and come to understand how my approach works.

In Chapter 7, I will address a number of common problems and offer suggestions for discovering what dynamic may be playing itself out and what you might do about it. This will just scratch the surface, but it will give you a sense of how complex, dynamic, and fun working with animals can be.

COMING HOME TO OUR LARGER FAMILY

As you stop anthropomorphizing and projecting human ideas onto your canine companion and start to see them for the unique, amazing being they really are, you may find yourself extending the same curiosity and understanding to the world beyond you and your dog. You may find yourself giving the benefit of the doubt to others more often, or you may feel a deep connection to the plight of wildlife in a distant country. You may even come to the realization that all species have an equal right to live out their purpose without harm.

Just from learning to see the world through the eyes of your dog? Yes. I have seen it happen many times.

As a species, humans have become deeply disconnected from one another and our planet. The only way we can mow down forests, contaminate our waters, spray our food with so many chemicals, treat animals the way we do in industrial agriculture, and exploit human lives for cheap goods is by distancing ourselves from these things. If we put ourselves over here, and think that those things are happening over there, outside of us, then we can believe it does not have anything to do with us. If we lived from the truth that humans are an integral part of the very ecosystem, we would not treat nature so blithely.

As your relationship with your dog grows and your personal practices make you more aware of the individual experience of others in the world around you, you will develop a deep appreciation for what animals can do that humans cannot. They can soar high overhead, see beyond the colors of the rainbow, breathe underwater, hear infrasound waves, navigate in the dark, lift hundreds of times their body weight, and regenerate limbs. You will see that while we are not all equal in our capacities and capabilities, that does not make any of us less important than others.

We do not need more training to get dogs to behave the way we want them to. We need more understanding and connection. From this place of respect, reciprocity, and mutuality, we have a chance to change not just our dog's behavior problems, but truly to change the world.

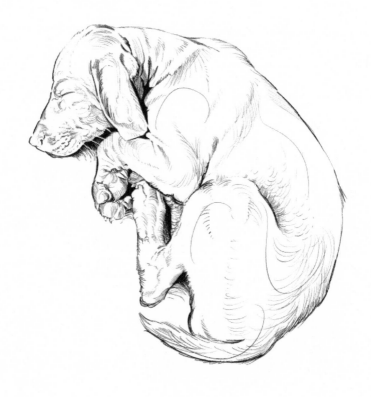

Security and safety—as well as being cared for and provided with everything you need for a fulfilling life—come directly from the hearts of those who love you. You will never create a sense of home with money or a four-walled structure with a roof.

—David J. Kurlander

1

Home is Where the Heart Is

The human/canine bond is like no other. Our close connection goes back tens of thousands of years, and we have evolved to live together to the mutual benefit of both our species. Over that time, dogs developed an uncanny ability to engage with us on a deep emotional level, and their presence in our lives and our families brings us enormous joy. Dogs have a profound impact on our emotional and physical lives—they can reduce our fear and anxiety levels, lower blood pressure and heart rate, help us live longer, and reduce our number of visits to the doctor. Having a furry companion in our life also helps us become more trusting, social, and happy.

I like to say humans and canines are the greatest love story that has ever existed. Living with a dog is the embodiment of the phrase *home is where the heart is*. They are family members as sure as our partners and children are also family members. As pack animals, they do not care much about their external environment. They do not mind if they are indoors or out, at home or in the car, as long as they are with us. As long as the integrity of the pack is maintained and their expectations are met, they will feel productive, safe, and secure, and reward us with their love, attention, and devotion. This bond is unlike any other. It is unbreakable to the core as they walk by our side through the trials and tribulations of life.

I have shared my life with many dogs. In the Introduction, you met Brandy, my childhood protector, and companion. Later in my teens and twenties, there was Nanuk, my 98-pound, black and tan Doberman pinscher who kept me safe on numerous occasions as I navigated through the Bronx. He had an uncanny knack for knowing which people in my life were honest and which ones were deceitful. There was a running joke among my small circle of friends that Nanuk was the first line of defense before meeting my parents. The funny part was that this was not so far from the truth. Nanuk decided who I should date and who was and was not allowed in my presence. Interestingly, he was never wrong.

Then there was Riley, my American bulldog. Fate brought us together as if someone above was watching over the both of us that day. I will never forget the moment I saw him behind the grimy chain link fence of a kennel. My goal that day was to perform a behavior evaluation on a dog that a friend was interested in adopting. As I walked down a narrow pathway with occupied kennels on either side of me, the smell and noise from barking dogs were overwhelming. But just before I reached the kennel of the dog I was planning to review, something happened. It was as if a divine hand reached down from the sky and compelled me to stop and look to my right.

The instant I laid eyes on him, I knew he was coming home with me. There he was, in this disgrace of a kennel, turned toward the concrete wall with his head held low as to hide his face. His poor skinny body and yellow-stained fur quickly ushered tears to my eyes. Riley became the sweetest and most docile pup I have ever lived with. Despite an early life of terrible abuse, he was a gentle and trusting soul. I have pictures of him a few months before he died—my two-year-old son Bjørn with his hand in Riley's mouth trying to take the dog's bone, and Riley patiently tolerating the little human-pup of our pack. With an immense heartbreak to the pack, Riley passed at the young age of 11 from liver cancer. Our pack has not been the same since.

My deepest connection was with my best hunting companion, a beautiful Labrador retriever called Cinder. We were like one in the field. He would trot in front of me about ten to twenty feet, his body moving forward and side to side, keeping a steady pace and rhythm, guided by his nose. When he would finally catch a scent in the air, he would freeze up like a statue and hold a steady point to the wind. Looking at me out of the corner of his eye, with wordless communication he would say, "Hey, there is something over there," and he was correct every single time.

When we were in the field, the connection was perfect, blissful, and almost primal.

Cinder was my shadow not only in the hunting field but also at work. He traveled with me every day, from town to town, county to county, state to state, up and down the east coast as we visited families who needed our help with behavior issues. Cinder was the perfect work partner. He knew every one of our routines and often performed them without asking. If the situation we encountered required the presence of a non-reactive dog, then Cinder would perform by not making eye contact and simply ignoring the other dog's negative communication. If the situation required an active, more engaging dog to help bring out a hidden personality, he would lead the way. He assisted with the rehabilitation of thousands of dogs in his lifetime. He helped settle the aggressive, quell the fearful, and teach manners to young rambunctious puppies who simply needed guidance from one of their own. He passed at the young age of 12 from kidney failure due to a tick-borne disease.

Today our pack includes three dogs: Kuno the Braque du Bourbonnais, Malachi the Bracco Italiano, and Ásgeirr the Labrador retriever. They are all hunting dogs being trained to work at competitive levels, and they are all integral members of our family, living among myself, my wife, and our four kids. Just like our human family members, each of these dogs brings their own personality to the mix, making for a lively and loving home. If you imagine your dog fitting seamlessly into your life the way mine have and do, but the reality is quite different, do not despair. This book will give you the tools to create a strong, harmonious pack. It will help you to create your own magical story of love, connection, and heroic acts. It will explain how to see the world through your dog's eyes, how to consider what they might be thinking or feeling, and how to act with that in mind so you can live a peaceful life together. It will give you the means to discover the elements found deep within the heart and soul of your dog that make them unique. It all starts with an emotional connection.

CONNECTING TO OUR ANIMAL BROTHERS AND SISTERS

Many animals have sophisticated ways of connecting and communicating with others of their species. Elephants, dolphins, bees, ants, birds, apes, and others have complex ways of "talking" to each other. We often forget that we are animals too, with an extremely sophisticated way of relating to each other that includes overt and subtle sounds, gestures, glances, and body language. On its surface, it seems that communicating person-to-person should be pretty straightforward, but as we are reminded from time to time through disagreements with friends and family (or even between nations and cultures), we are not always on the same page.

While many species "talk" amongst themselves, interspecies communication is rare. It is so unusual, in fact, that humans find such interactions captivating. We love videos that feature friendships between a cat and a bird, a turtle and a cow, a tiger and a pig, a sheep and an elephant—the list goes on. Occasionally we hear about an unusual interspecies relationship between a human and another animal, and we marvel. Take Koko the gorilla and Alex the parrot as examples.

Koko the gorilla (1971–2018) was born and raised in captivity and could understand with more than 1,000 gestures based on American Sign Language. She had a sophisticated use of language and was said to talk about memories, make jokes, and even invent new words. Besides her caregiver, Francine Patterson, she had a number of cats as friends after asking for one of her own for Christmas in 1983.

Alex the African gray parrot (1976–2007) proved that it is not just primates that can communicate with us. Alex had up to 100 vocalizations of objects, colors, and actions. He was able to solve puzzles and was known to ask questions, including once querying, "What color?" while looking at himself in the mirror.

Alex could do simple math and even seemed to understand the concept of zero.

As impressive as Koko and Alex were, gorillas and parrots (and dolphins, elephants, cats, etc.) do not communicate with us with the same level of sophistication as dogs. They also do not integrate into our lives in the same way. We cannot share our couch with a gorilla while we binge watch our latest favorite show. We cannot play a game of frisbee with an elephant. We cannot bundle the parrot into the car with the kids for a weekend at the beach. On the other hand, we can welcome dogs into nearly every part of our life, and we have for tens of thousands of years.

COMMUNICATING WITH OUR FURRY FRIENDS

I have worked with and acquired countless species of animal beings—such as tortoises, lizards, snakes, spiders, birds, and a variety of small mammals—yet there is only one species that has become an active, participatory member of my family: the dog. With somewhere between 70 to 90 million dogs living in about 38% of households in the United States, I am clearly not alone in my love for our furry family members. Over millennia, they have learned how to read us and how to communicate what they want or need. Clearly, it is working, but since they do not "talk" to us using words, how exactly does that communication happen? Emotion.

Marc Bekoff, author of *The Emotional Lives of Animals,* says, "Lacking a shared language, emotions are perhaps our most effective means of cross-species communication. We can share our emotions, we can understand the language of feelings, and that is why we form deep and enduring social bonds with many other beings. Emotions are the glue that binds."

In his book *The Expression of the Emotions in Man and Animals,* Charles Darwin, ever the keen observer of animal behavior, explores how animals express emotion in a remarkably similar way to humans. He tells a story of one of his family dogs, whose emotional state could change on a dime when he was redirected during his daily walks. Darwin writes, "I formerly possessed a large dog, who, like every other dog, was much pleased to go out walking. He showed his pleasure by trotting gravely before me with high steps, head much raised, moderately erected ears, and tail carried aloft but not stiffly."

Partway through his walk, Darwin would often take a turn off the path to visit a greenhouse, at which point his dog would make clear his displeasure: "This was always a great disappointment to the dog, as he did not know whether I should continue my walk.... His look of dejection was known to every member of the family and was called his *hot-house face*. This consisted in the head drooping much, the whole body sinking a little and remaining motionless; the ears and tail falling suddenly down, but the tail was by no means wagged. With the falling of the ears and of his great chaps, the eyes became much changed in appearance, and I fancied that they looked less bright. His aspect was that of piteous, hopeless dejection; and it was, as I have said, laughable, as the cause was so slight."

While written in the style of the times (it was published in 1872) and with heavy-handed anthropomorphism (projecting human characteristics onto another species, which we will talk about more in the next chapter), Darwin's observations demonstrate a number of ways that dogs communicate with us: through gestures (of ears and tail), carriage, body language, and gaze. Eye contact is a critical means of communication for humans. We bond with each other by looking into each other's eyes. When we do, it releases a hormone called oxytocin—also known as the "love hormone"—that plays a role in bonding between a mother and baby and in the development of trust. Beyond child-rearing, oxytocin is generated when any two people make a deep connection.

Dogs, it turns out, have the same reaction to eye contact as people. Several studies have shown that when a human and dog interact in a positive way—through play and eye contact—the levels of oxytocin go up in both. A study by Takefumi Kikusui, an animal behaviorist at Azabu University in Sagamihara, Japan, found that dog's levels increased up to 130%, while humans got an extra-big dose of "feel good," with an increase of up to 300%.

While many animals glance at us long enough to be able to recognize our face (and possibly even identify us as a particular individual), no other animal makes and sustains eye contact as often or as long as our companion dogs. Even wild dogs and wolves make less frequent eye contact, and they do not hold that eye contact for as long. With some animals, like gorillas and leopards, eye contact can be taken as a sign of aggression.

In addition to eye contact, dogs have the unique capacity to know where to look when we point at something (or when we do something like turn off the path and orient ourselves in the direction of the greenhouse). No other animal—not even the chimpanzee, our closest relative, or the wolf, the dog's close relative—can understand pointing the way dogs do. Puppies from as young as six weeks old can follow the gesture, and when it is combined with a vocalization with an agreeable tone of voice, a dog is even more likely to follow our pointing. Whether the dog's long evolutionary history with humans caused them to evolve this skill or it is something they learn quickly as they grow up has been a debate for decades. Like all good nature versus nurture arguments, it is probably a little bit of both.

One of the more interesting evolutionary developments in dogs that allows them to communicate better with us is the appearance of the levator anguli oculi medialis muscle. That is the facial muscle that allows your dog to raise their eyebrows in that quizzical, melt-your-heart expression that makes you think they are hanging on your every word. Wolves, for the most part, do not have this muscle (notably, neither do Siberian Huskies). But most of our companion dogs do, and, as moved as we are by these expressions, it is likely we subconsciously selected for this trait in breeding. What the expression means, exactly, is still unclear, but it has the effect of making a dog's eyes look bigger, which we tend to read as a sign of sadness—though of course, it is tremendously difficult for us to know for sure what a dog is feeling or thinking.

Darwin does not mention whether his dog lodged a verbal protest over his thwarted walks, but vocalizations are another common way dogs communicate among themselves and with humans. Interestingly, barking seems to be a result of domestication; wolves and wild dogs rarely bark. They make plenty of noises to communicate with each other, and we are all familiar with the howl of a pack of wolves or coyotes, but they do not bark the way our companion dogs do.

There have not been many studies to look at what dogs are communicating when they bark, but the research that has been done indicates humans are quite good at deciphering canine-speak. One study showed people are able to distinguish between aggressive, playful, and fearful barks whether they had a dog companion in their life or not. A different study revealed that babies as young as six months old can tell the difference between an aggressive or a friendly bark. Combined, these results suggest a deep evolutionary connection between our species.

Evidence of this connection continues to be revealed as science is now able to peer into the mind of the dog using various imaging techniques. One study showed that dogs' brains respond most strongly to the smell of a familiar human as opposed to smells of an unfamiliar human or familiar or unfamiliar canines. A different study indicated that dogs process auditory sounds in the same part of the brain where humans do. It appears that in many ways, our dog's brain may be hardwired to connect with us.

LENDING US THEIR SENSES

With the capacity to communicate with such nuance, it would be tempting to assume dogs see the world just like we do. Yes, dogs may have been by our side for as long as we can remember, and yes, they may communicate with us in a way no other species does, but their way of seeing the world is unique and non-human, despite our close connection. Understanding that dogs have a dog-like way of perceiving the world is key to working with our canine companions in a respectful way.

One of the biggest ways we can honor that relationship is by understanding that dogs possess abilities far beyond our own and that we have benefited greatly from those abilities, especially from their sense of smell. Dogs are estimated to have a sense of smell at least 10,000 times stronger than ours. They can be trained to help with search and rescue operations on land and in water, including locating people in natural disasters, lost children or elderly, and homicide victims. Some dogs are specially trained to sniff out bombs, drugs, gas leaks, bed bugs, and even sewage leaks, also known as Illicit Discharge Detection and Elimination (I.D.D.E), to help save our environment. Others are able to detect human diseases like cancer, Parkinson's, epilepsy, diabetes, and tuberculosis, to name a few.

Dogs can even lend us their senses without being trained. Nanuk, the Doberman who was so protective of me, also adored my mother. He was like her shadow, following her around incessantly, even sleeping in the bed with her on occasion. At one point he started poking her in the ribs with his nose. He did this for a number of months, developing what seemed like a strange obsession with this part of her body. Despite Nanuk's persistence, my mom was not sure what he wanted, so she disregarded this strange idiosyncrasy, and mildly corrected him by expressing her disapproval.

A pre-op appointment before a hernia surgery eventually brought my mother to the doctor for a scan. With a little voice of concern whispering in her ear, she insisted the doctor increase the area of the scan to include her lower ribs where Nanuk had been poking her for many months. When the results came back, we learned that there was a grape-sized cancerous tumor in her lung, just beneath the spot he was obsessed with. Luckily, the cancer was only stage one, and she is now cancer-free because of our special bond with that dog. I never trained him to detect cancer, but his sensitivity—and his love and devotion to his pack—saved her life.

Another area where dogs lend us their senses, and have been for millennia, is hunting. We borrow their ability to track and chase down prey, and together we are able to hunt more successfully than either of us alone. It is entirely arguable that humans would not have survived or flourished as we have without dogs and their willingness to share their gifts so freely. There are countless animals with amazing capabilities, yet none so ready to share them as the dog.

CREATING A RECIPROCAL RELATIONSHIP—DOING OUR PART

As they have done for tens of thousands of years, dogs continue to make our lives better, longer, and more satisfying—no questions asked. In return, our part of the deal is to create the best environment for them to live in. A key question we need to ask is, "What do they expect from us?"

When we welcome a dog into our life, we bring them into our pack. As the leader of the pack, our responsibility is to provide what our dog needs to fulfill their purpose. Most domestic dogs (though not all) need us to provide food, shelter, and safety in our human-created environment. Like humans, dogs require basic necessities to flourish in the pack. But, most notably, they must be allowed to contribute to the solidarity of the pack in some way.

Each dog has a unique individual personality that expresses a specific purpose, and it is up to us as the provider to discover and understand what that purpose is and help them satisfy it. Herding dogs are hunters. They provide for the pack; that is their purpose. If I have welcomed a herding dog into my house but I live in an urban area, I need to think about how I can satisfy that dog's need to provide.

Too often in my work, I have seen people have unrealistic expectations of their dogs. Asking a Border collie to live in a tiny studio apartment in New York City or a Chihuahua to live in an Alaskan winter is asking a dog to exist in conditions they were never meant to experience. Expecting a high energy dog to spend all day home alone only for you to be too tired to take them for a walk in the evening is bound to create an unhappy dog who is likely to act out. Moreover, it is unrealistic to assume they can tell the difference between a street tree or Mr. McGregor's prized garden when they look for a place to relieve themselves unless we have set that expectation for them.

We cannot expect what we perceive as good behavior from our dogs without making allowance for their needs. If you require your dog to perform and all you do is demand without giving back, the relationship is likely to have significant problems, just as any other relationship would. A successful relationship, whether canine or human, is built on mutual respect. If you give your dog time and attention, observe their behavior, and get curious about how they see the world, you are far more likely to have a happy and well-adjusted pup even before you do any kind of training.

I often hear people refer to themselves as a "pet owner" and I encourage my clients to drop this language. To own another being sets up an imbalanced power dynamic, a master and servant situation that prevents us from appreciating the unique perspective that a dog has to offer the world and from connecting with them more deeply. I suggest you think of your dog in some ways like you do your child. They need your guidance to navigate in this human-created world—they need assistance interpreting the labyrinthine rules of an alien society. We brought these animals into our world, and we owe them at least that.

Dogs are not human, but they are emotional beings who deserve a certain amount of allowance for their own desires and needs. Let's say you get to know your dog's personality, and you learn they are cautious around new people. Much like if you had a child who was hesitant around new people, it is your job to protect that dog and modulate their interactions with strangers. In the same way you would not let a random stranger simply walk up and hug your child, violating their personal space and wishes for privacy, you can keep people from approaching your dog uninvited.

If you do not step up and meet your dog's needs in this way and allow such an interaction to occur, that communicates to the dog that you do not understand their needs or you just do not consider them important. Either way, you are not responding how they expect their provider to respond, and they may react with fear or some maladaptive behavior. They will not understand if you punish them for acting out in self-defense when you were the one to violate their trust by not protecting them. Your dog has the right to not be petted if they do not want it, and your job is to get to know your dog well enough to be able to act as interpreter.

Today we tend to think that training is the answer to all our dog's "problems," but our emotional connection is all that really matters. We bonded successfully for thousands of years before humans came up with formalized dog training. Take the time to get inside your dog's mind and understand their needs, then do your best to respect and fulfill those needs, and you will see positive results.

As we develop this new kind of relationship with the canines in our life, we gradually come to recognize that all life forms have a purpose, experience emotion, breathe, bleed, feel fear, and as such, deserve our respect. Dogs can help us let go of our human superiority complex and teach us how to coexist and nurture this world that provides us with so much. Without nature, without all the other forms of life on this planet—from animals to plants to water—we would perish. Our deep connection with our canine companions offers us this reminder.

HOW DID THIS RELATIONSHIP COME TO BE?

If the human/canine relationship is the greatest love story ever written, when did we meet, and how did we come to develop such a deep bond? It is hard to believe, but the answer to that question is hidden back in time somewhere. Today, scientists do their best to piece together clues, proposing theories about how we got from the wolf to the domesticated dog, but the more we know, the muddier the picture becomes.

We have been writing things down for about 5,000 years, but we have evidence of dogs and humans living together much further back than that. One popular theory is that wolves would hang around human settlements waiting for scraps to be tossed away on the outskirts of the village or camp. Some of them would venture close to people, and over time the courageous ones would begin to form relationships with humans, protecting the settlement in exchange for food. Eventually, the people started breeding the wolves for the traits they found desirable.

This is a romantic story, but is it likely to have happened? Could humans have forced the hand of genetic evolution through selective breeding? While it is possible humans could have figured out that breeding two tamer wolves gives you a better chance at having baby wolves that are more tame, I tend to doubt this theory simply due to a lack of knowledge of reproduction and genetics tens of thousands of years ago. It requires a level of sophisticated understanding that I think is unlikely.

Additionally, in recent years, DNA evidence has deflated the wolf-to-dog theory by showing that gray wolves and wild dogs split from a now-extinct wolf species between 20,000 to 40,000 years ago. Our domestic dogs came from this split, but there are no wild packs of Golden retrievers or Doberman pinscher roaming the forests, so how did we get from wild dogs to living side by side with our furry friends? Where did it happen? How did the relationship form?

Some theories propose that the wild dog was domesticated more than once, while others suggest they were domesticated in more than one location. There is evidence for both of these theories, but there are also many gaps in the story that remain to be filled in. What we do know is that for millennia, cultures around the world have shared a deep bond with dogs.

The oldest evidence of a possible link between humans and dogs comes from ancient cave art in Spain and Gibraltar. Naturalist Bernie Taylor, author of *Before Orion,* hypothesizes that representations of animals in the Cave of El Castillo and Gorham's Cave resemble dogs, some of which we might recognize today. The Chauvet Cave in France has preserved footprints from a young child alongside a dog that date to 26,000 years ago.

In China, there is archaeological evidence that dogs and humans coexisted about 15,000 years ago. Along with being hunters and protectors, they were seen as a defense against bad spirits, and their iconography eventually morphed into the "foo-dog," the lion-like dog statues that adorn the entry of many Chinese buildings. Dogs are also the 11th sign in the Chinese zodiac, and while they fell out of favor as pets in China in the mid-20th century, they are growing in popularity once more.

The ancient Egyptians revered domesticated dogs, burying them with humans as well as in dedicated dog cemeteries. From their records, we know many of their dogs' names (Brave One, Reliable, North Wind), and from their illustrations, we know they used collars and leashes with dogs. Dogs also held the highest of roles within their religion, as the Egyptian god Anubis illustrates, and were a prevalent part of daily life as hunters, protectors, and companions.

Dogs were also an important part of life in ancient Greece and figured into their mythology in many ways, including as the three-headed dog Cerberus who guarded the gates of Hades. Ptolemy was the first to record the names of the two constellations represented as dogs following Orion through the sky, Canis major and Canis minor. Canes venatici, named in the 17th century, forms Chara and Asterion, the dogs associated with the nearby constellation of Boötes the hunter.

Even while we cannot know the origin of our life together, we can see that dogs have been our companions throughout time. In the 19th century, breeding began in earnest, giving us the incredible variety of dogs we have today (depending on who is counting, there are anywhere from 150 to 450 breeds). Between that accelerated tinkering with traits and an experiment done on foxes in Russia in the early 1960s, we have some insight into what traits emerge when we choose to breed for animals that live amicably with us—floppy ears, smaller teeth, wider eyes, a shorter snout, and a generally more puppy-like appearance, even into adulthood.

What this means to me is that we have a responsibility to our canine friends. We have created them, we have brought them into our world, and we should do our best to understand and meet their needs. In return, we get the benefit of their unconditional

love and devotion and all the joy they bring to our lives.

Discovering your ability to let go of personal thoughts, emotions, and social norms is a feat worth pursuing. Unencumbered by preconceptions, you can more easily see through the eyes of another, which is an enlightening and life-changing experience.

—David J. Kurlander

2
Shifting Your Perception

Imagine you move into a shared house where your new housemates welcome you with excitement and give you gifts to make you feel comfortable. There is the usual awkwardness of being in a new environment around unfamiliar people, but generally things seem promising. You learn something new each day about what is expected of you, and you gradually start to relax and let a little more of your personality come through. Your housemates also get more comfortable with your presence, and everyone falls into a routine.

But then you come down to the kitchen for breakfast one day and your coffee is gone. You look for your coat where you hung it up the night before and find it on the couch in the living room. Because you respect your housemates and feel a connection to them, you make an effort to communicate your concerns. You try different ways of speaking up and reaching out—leaving a note, sending a text—but their response is dismissive.

After a few months of trying to communicate your frustration and confusion over these small incongruencies, you finally confront your housemates in person, expressing how upset you are because one of them ate the special cupcake a friend had bought you for your birthday. Instead of admitting blame, they misinterpret your behavior as aggressive and threatening. You do not understand this because your attempts to communicate subtly but clearly have gone unnoticed for some time now, and you thought telling them directly would work, but it feels like they are speaking a different language and playing by a different set of rules. Now imagine they sought the advice of a specialist who suggested you be disciplined and possibly medicated for your behavior. Luckily, as a human, you can walk away from this situation. Our canine companions cannot.

What we see as behavior issues are often a dog's attempts at communicating with us that, in some way, they are not getting what they need. If we are going to bring them into our homes and integrate them into our lives, then we owe them the courtesy of trying to understand what they are telling us. We do not have to stop thinking and perceiving like the human beings we are (we cannot, after all), but we do need to open our minds to the idea that other animal beings have their own ways of seeing the world. In fact, within all species, there is a tremendous variation in the way we perceive things. Our senses—the organs by which we perceive our environment—are oriented to what evolution determined was important to keep us alive. The capacity to hear infrasound (like elephants), read the world with infrared-sensitive receptors (like some species of bats or snakes), or discern minute scents at the levels canines can were not skills necessary for our survival, so we did not evolve to experience the world in the same way they do.

Our particular way of perceiving the world, combined with our ability to verbalize, conceptualize, and develop structures, allowed our species to proliferate in a vastly different manner than that of any other species on earth. In this process, we made a tragic error: we equated that exponential growth with superiority, and we forgot our place in the larger ecosystem. For millennia, we existed as part of a complex web of nature whose balance ensured our survival and growth as a species. We had a symbiotic relationship with the land and animal beings around us, including canines, who helped us survive and thrive by being our herding, hunting, and protective companions.

As technology advanced and we no longer needed to remain attuned to nature for our survival, we forgot our roots. Today, our kids think heat comes from adjusting the thermostat on the wall; food comes from the refrigerator, a restaurant, or the grocery store; and the only way to get around is by way of vehicles parked in our driveways. While a few people chop wood for heat, grow food to eat, or get where they need to go by the power of their own two feet, almost all of us have forgotten the source of all these luxuries: the natural world of which we are apart. And our addiction to endless consumption leads us to do terrible things to our world, sacrificing ethics and humanity in a quest for inexpensive fake food, low gas prices, endless monetary growth, or the latest new technology.

REMEMBERING OUR PLACE IN THE WEB OF NATURE

What does all this have to do with your dog's behavior? I firmly believe that a good relationship with our canine companions is dependent on us shifting away from thinking of ourselves as the top of the food chain and remembering that we are a part of a delicate circle of life on this planet. We must recognize that we share this world with other emotional beings who contribute to the life and beauty of this planet too, not just dogs. Other animals, insects, plant life, and even water all have their own way of interacting with the world—their own perspective if you will. Luckily, working on your relationship with your dog is the perfect way to reconnect with nature and recalibrate your place in the world.

Dogs connect to the environment in a way we cannot—we will never experience the world as they do—but they communicate through emotion in ways that we can understand if we try. Sometimes we get the message right away: when a dog shows their teeth, lowers their head, and growls at you, the hair on the back of your neck stands up and your stomach knots with fear. No need for words or interpretation in this case! We have the potential to apprehend what dogs are communicating anytime. As we attune to their emotions more clearly, we can become more sensitive to the world around us in general. Their in-the-moment response to the environment can help us realize our weaknesses and sense our disconnection from the world. Not so we can feel bad about it, but so we can find our way back to connection through them.

In the distant past, when we lived in harmony with the environment, we were also in sync with our canine friends, hunting or herding together to the benefit of both species. That relationship lasted tens of thousands of years before we began to keep dogs just as pets. When the industrial revolution rolled through in the late 1800s, our lives moved indoors into factories and offices, and we forgot our connection to the environment. Much like it became a status symbol to not have to work, it was also a sign of your wealth if your dog did not have to work either. At this point, our canine companions were only required to be cute and behave. There were, of course, still some dogs kept for working, and plenty of dogs roamed the streets without homes, but generally speaking, dogs became a status symbol.

When we retired dogs from their useful role as hunters and providers and began to treat them as mindless beasts, the harmony we once lived in was disrupted. Having not been bred to play this new role, we needed to coax them with food or bully them with punishment and painful devices to break their spirit, bend their will, and get them to do what we want them to do. This approach to "training," or what some may call "behavior modification," became more prevalent as we began to ask them to do more unnatural things like stay in the house all day or walk only on a leash. Many modern-day training methods work from the assumption that the human is the master, and the canine is the servant, stripping them of their participation in providing for their pack while simultaneously devaluing their existence. At worst, this thinking allows us to perpetrate terrible abuse; at best, it has us miss out on a deeper and more authentic connection with these magnificent beings.

I propose we take a step back from what we think we know and open our minds to the possibility that our dog's way of seeing the world is as valid as our own. Like us, each dog has their own personality, perspective, and unique life experience. Like every other conscious living being, they each have a basic set of expectations that allows them to flourish as they progress through life. If they cannot fulfill those expectations—if their needs are not met—fear and anxiety will set in, and they will likely behave in ways that are disruptive or disorderly.

MARLEY THE URBAN HUNTER

My clients, Nathan and Alexandra, live in a third-floor apartment in New York City with their German shorthaired pointer Marley. A handsome dog, Marley came from a prestigious lineage of upland bird hunters vetted by the North American Versatile Hunting Dog Association (NAVHDA). This extremely dedicated young couple reached out to me after many failed attempts to try to work with Marley. Their primary complaints were that at six months Marley was still not housebroken and that a simple walk could take them up to an hour because Marley would freeze up and stare at every pigeon, squirrel, or blowing leaf they encountered. When they would attempt to pull on his leash to press on with the walk, Marley would lunge forward and pounce at his target.

Nathan and Alexandra were busy entrepreneurs who were happy to make time to walk and play with Marley a couple of times a day, but they did not have the flexibility required to take him outside for an extended duration of time. They were also considering having a baby and were concerned that his lunging behavior might be a sign of aggression. As soon as I met them and heard their story, I realized we had a "miscommunicating housemates" situation on our hands.

Marley has a genetic predisposition for hunting. It is in the very fabric of who he is. Living in an apartment in Manhattan was not the situation his genetic inheritance prepared him for. When he would get those few hours outside each day, his underused hunting instincts would kick into high gear. Finally, he could be who he was! He would have so much fun pointing and hunting the city's wildlife that he would forget to go to the bathroom. Later, back in the apartment with no distractions or stimulation—and unfortunately no one around to let him out—he could not hold it any longer and would have no choice but to relieve himself indoors.

Much like our housemate situation, humans and canines were at a crossroads. Luckily for this family, I did not suggest discipline or medication for Marley. Redirecting him with food or using drugs or elaborate devices would only divert or disable his natural behavior—it would not fundamentally change who he is. Since my philosophy is that every being has an inherent right to be who they are and to live their purpose, I helped Nathan and Alexandra understand who Marley is at his core. I encouraged them to assume the role of provider and figure out how they could give Marley ways to realize his potential and feel like he is contributing to the pack. While it is an added challenge to help guide him and satisfy his impulses in the midst of an urban environment, it is not impossible. And it is the only way that everyone in the family would get to live a happy life where they can be unapologetically who they are.

We bring these beautiful beings into our lives and expect them to live in a foreign environment that revolves around humans. Most dogs' expectations are never met, and their frustration rises to sometimes uncontrollable levels. This is where we have to consider the safety and happiness of all that surrounds us. If we can find our way to communicating with our canine companions on their terms—or at least learn to understand their needs and fulfill them—then ninety-nine percent of the time behavior issues disappear.

KEEP YOUR PROJECTIONS IN CHECK

A primary way we stifle our canine companions' individuality is by projecting human traits onto them in a process called anthropomorphism. Projection is a psychological term that is worth unpacking, as it may offer some helpful insight into your life and relationships beyond the one with your dog.

The concept of projection is not new. Early Greek philosophers wrote about how our thoughts influence how we see others, and most major religions address the idea in one way or another. But it was Sigmund Freud (1856-1939), the founder of psychoanalysis, who clearly articulated the phenomenon as an unconscious psychological defense mechanism wherein we take the parts of ourselves that we deem unacceptable and "project" them onto others. For example, if we cannot own that we are irresponsible, we claim someone else is. If we cannot acknowledge our own anxiety, we will tend to say others are anxious.

While Freud suggested it was just the negative things about ourselves that we offload onto others, over time, the idea of projection has come to include ascribing to others whatever thoughts, feelings, or motivations are going on inside us— positive, negative, or neutral. And it is widely accepted that we do not just project onto other people—we also project onto ethnic groups, organizations or businesses, political parties, inanimate objects (from toys to trees), spiritual figures (like gods and goddesses), and, of course, animals.

There is no doubt that being able to imagine life as experienced through the minds of others is an important skill to have as a human being. It is the basis of empathy and understanding, and it allows us to form bonds within our own species. But it can very easily go awry when we make assumptions about another person's experience based on our own.

For example, let us say you visit a store and need some assistance. You walk up to the first salesperson you see and notice that their brow is furrowed and they are frowning. Intimidated, you decide not to ask for assistance. Instead, you leave the store and call your friend and complain to them about the unfriendly and grumpy salesperson. You get more and more worked up, saying that everyone in that store is always unfriendly and that you are never going to shop there again because the whole company itself is a menace to the world!

Can you see who is the grumpy and unfriendly one in this scenario? (Hint: it is not the salesperson!) In this case, you are projecting characteristics onto the person, the store, and the entire company that you do not know are accurate. There is no way of knowing if the salesperson's furrowed brow meant unfriendliness since you did not actually speak to them. Perhaps they just had an argument with their boss, maybe they recently lost their canine companion and were fighting back tears, or maybe they simply had gas and did not feel well for a second.

When we anthropomorphize the dogs in our life, we project our ideas and emotions onto them in much the same way as this example with the salesperson. We assume that their mental, emotional, and psychological world is identical to ours, and we assume they will behave like we would in a given situation. But they are not human—they are perfect, complex, and beautiful beings who act precisely as nature intended them to. They are receiving a different set of data than we are, and their responses will, inevitably, not match ours.

Expecting dogs to behave like us sets them up to fail and sets us up to feel frustrated. And when we are frustrated, our first impulse is to blame them. Why won't he stop barking? Why does she chew all the furniture? Why doesn't he get along with other dogs? When confronted with these behaviors, if we are projecting our human experience onto them, we tend to assume their pathology is the same as ours and we diagnose them with anxiety, depression, separation disorder, or obsessive-compulsive disorder. Unfortunately, many dogs are then medicated for these "issues." And if that fails, some even pay the ultimate price and are euthanized for their behavior.

I am not saying that dogs do not have emotions or that they do not behave badly sometimes. In fact, dogs are pure emotion. If a dog's human companion dies, they certainly experience that loss. If they are left alone all day, they undoubtedly feel isolation and insecurity. But they experience emotions differently than we do, and we cannot just apply our human psychology (or our prescription drugs) to their experience. Psychology is not linear. The framework of human psychology is only one way of seeing things, so do not let it define your dog's experience. Dogs have their own way of seeing the world, and each dog will navigate the world differently depending on their individual personality, genetics, and the experiences they have had.

CLIVE THE "RESENTFUL" COONHOUND

Here is a story that illustrates how easy it is to project our feelings onto our animal companions. One day I received a phone call from a client looking for help with her 18-month-old Redbone coonhound named Clive. The woman, we will call her Juliet, explained that her dog had been psychologically damaged by her recent separation from her husband Joe. She suggested that Clive was so resentful over the separation that he had turned aggressive toward her. She even went so far as to imply that the dog was continuing the cycle of abuse that she had experienced with her husband.

Since I know dogs do not have the same kind of motivations as a disgruntled or abusive spouse (this was a projection on my client's part), I investigated further. It turns out that Joe had been Clive's primary caretaker. Clive often went to work with Joe, and on average they spent more than 75% of each day together. At home, Joe groomed, walked, and fed Clive. They spent weekends working in the yard, and every night Clive slept on Joe's side of the bed. In Clive's eyes, Joe was the primary provider for everything he needed to survive and thrive.

With this information, I was able to explain to Juliet that Clive's aggressive outbursts were not stemming from deep-rooted resentment (like a human child's behavior might). Instead, his actions were a result of the restructuring of the family. With his primary provider gone, Clive was looking for some way to reintroduce balance into the pack. His actions were an attempt to communicate that there was a leadership vacuum and either he or Juliet needed to fill it. By misunderstanding the motivation of his actions, Juliet was leaving his request for clarity about the pack structure unanswered, and Clive was acting out in frustration and desperation. Once she understood what Clive was trying to say and applied a set of practical routines to answer his questions and assure him of his new role in the pack order, the situation quickly resolved.

Jungian psychoanalyst James Hollis says that in order to develop a relationship of mutual respect, we need to examine "what kind of traffic" we are creating between us. He describes this as the first step to healing ourselves and clearing the obstacles that are standing in the way of a better, more honest, more authentic relationship. He was talking about human-to-human relationships, but the concept works for our relationship with our dogs as well. To have a mutually respectful relationship, Juliet had to examine what kind of traffic she was generating, in this case, her projections, and then be flexible enough to let those go and see the situation through Clive's eyes. Owning our projections and being able to take a different perspective on a situation is an indispensable life skill that will benefit both our human and canine relationships. The ability to let go of past psychological injuries will clear our path forward, allowing our minds to become more receptive to experience other potentials.

THE GENETICS OF TEMPERAMENT

One of the questions I get asked with some regularity is how much of a dog's behavior is predetermined by their genes. It is the classic nature versus nurture question, a puzzle science is still working to sort out. But we have come a long way to answering that question, beginning with the work of Konrad Lorenz, a 20th-century zoologist and founder of ethology, the study of animal behavior. Lorenz is best known for his studies of imprinting in birds, and his work was one of the main influences on the beginning of my journey on the path of learning about animal behavior.

Lorenz suggested that animals evolved to behave in whatever way would maximize the chances of survival for the species. For example, since it would greatly increase their chances of living to reproduce, geese evolved so the goslings imprint on their mother, attaching themselves to her and following her around. He demonstrated this process by showing himself (and honking like a goose) to some newly hatched goslings who quickly attached themselves to him and followed him around instead of their mother.

Because it happened automatically before a chick even ate its first food, Lorenz theorized that the action, or behavior, is inheritable and inevitable—it will happen regardless of the environment. Moreover, he said, all animals, not just geese, are born with certain instincts and are compelled to act them out. If they do not get the typical opportunities or prompts, the behavior will still happen—in this case, Lorenz became "mother" to a bunch of newly hatched geese as the goslings automatically acted out the imprinting behavior in the absence of their natural mother.

Like other animals, dogs too are born with genetically predisposed behavioral tendencies. Just like they are genetically predisposed to have a tan coat, brown eyes, or grow only to a certain size, they may also have an instinct to hunt, herd, or protect—as well as a tendency to be energetic or mellow. Behavior traits are more difficult to assess than physical characteristics as they typically involve a combination of a number of genes; it is easier to figure out how to breed for a tan coat, which is dependent on just a couple of genes. Regardless, over time, breeders have been able to select for temperament, which is why we can say, generally speaking, Jack Russell terriers are energetic and smart, Labrador retrievers are friendly and affectionate, and Akitas are courageous and loyal. Dogs in a particular breed do not just look alike—they are also likely to share some broad character traits based on their genetics.

In addition to their genetic predisposition, the individual personality of the dog and the environment they are raised in can also affect their behavior. We will explore more about breeds, temperaments, personalities, and environment in Chapter 3, but I introduce these ideas here to illustrate that your dog was born with a fundamental predisposition to certain behaviors. If your dog has the drive to hunt and is unable to fulfill that urge, they will find a way to act it out, whether that be stalking your cat, chasing your neighbor's chickens, or barking all day when left home alone. Knowing your dog's genetic predisposition can give you a good foundation for how to begin to see the world through their eyes.

LEAPING INTO THE QUANTUM FIELD

While biology continues to uncover and articulate the mysteries of genetics, the field of quantum physics gives us a different perspective. Each dog and family that I work with has a unique situation and requires a different approach, but they all share one thing in common: the "fix" begins with the people, not the dog.

If you wish your furry family member to behave differently, you will need to change your heart and your mind. Too often I encounter people who have given up hope. They have resigned themselves to the fact that this is how their dog behaves and that it has nothing to do with them. But your dog being able to reach their full potential has everything to do with you shedding the negativity bias you have assumed from a skeptical world. You must remove the shackles of the limiting beliefs and assumptions you have taken on, and only then, once you can see your canine companion's potential, will they respond accordingly.

In his book *The Seven Spiritual Laws of Success,* Deepak Chopra explains that the first law, the Law of Pure Potentiality, "is based on the fact that we are, in our essential state, pure consciousness. Pure consciousness is pure potentiality; it is the field of all possibilities and infinite creativity." According to Chopra, when you are able to access that state—when you spend time in the field of potentiality—you gain the "ability to fulfill any dream you have, because you are the eternal possibility, the immeasurable potential of all that was, is, and will be."

Time and time again I have witnessed people fail to communicate with their dogs, only to take the leash from them and within seconds have the dog do as I ask. It is not because I have any special authority or possess magical powers that my clients do not. I may have more experience, but the dog is not responding to my experience—they are responding to my state of mind. I do not approach them with the idea that they cannot do what I am asking. Instead, in my mind's eye, I hold the possibility that they can do it. The word "impossible" is not in my vocabulary, either for myself or for the dogs (or even people) I work with. Of course, I am not talking about asking the dogs to do biologically impossible things like fly or hoot like an owl. Rather, I consider their genetic heritage, I honor their individuality, and I connect to them in their language—emotion.

Working with your dog will typically require that you change your attitude. I do not mean just use the power of positive thinking; I am talking about quantum theory. In our old mechanistic way of seeing things, known as Newtonian physics, we can predict how forces act on matter. For example, we know if we throw the frisbee, our dog will either catch it or miss it based on how well they judge the velocity of our throw and whether they end up in just the right position at the right time to nab it out of the air. If we knew all the variables, we could easily plug them into an equation and get a yes or no answer. It is predictable. The frisbee will come down from the sky and it will be caught, or it will not be.

Quantum theory works with life at a much smaller level—the level of waves and particles. And once you get to that level, nothing is predictable. Let us look at the classic thought experiment used to explain this idea: Schrödinger's Cat. A physicist with wide-ranging curiosity, Erwin Schrödinger created this mental exercise as a way to think through when something becomes reality. Let me be clear, the experiment was not actually carried out—it was only imagined. And while Schrödinger used a cat, I am going to use a dog.

Imagine I put a puppy in a box with some silent gunpowder. (The original thought exercise imagined using a radioactive material, but Einstein and others imagined it using gunpowder, which we will use here.) The gunpowder has a 50% chance of blowing up and a 50% chance of not blowing up. Either way, because it is silent, and because we leave the room, we will not hear whether it goes off or not.

In the old way of thinking of things, if someone asked, we would say the gunpowder has exploded and the puppy is dead, or it has not, and the puppy is alive. But quantum theory says that until we open the box to see what has happened, our puppy is BOTH dead and alive at the same time. Both possibilities simultaneously exist. Once we open the box and observe the puppy's current state, all possibilities collapse down into the result, and we either see the puppy has died or it has survived. In one moment, all possibilities existed, and in the next there was only one outcome.

The idea that the puppy could be both alive and dead is known as superposition, or the state of pure potentiality. In that place, anything is possible. Deepak Chopra's field of potentiality, what he describes as our essential nature, is the same as quantum physics' superposition. From this place, there are infinite possibilities.

The idea of superposition and the field of potentiality can also be applied to our process of thinking. Just before you think a thought, there is a place where any thought is possible and where all options are on the table. In this place, nothing is set in stone. However, as soon as you think a thought, the energy of that thought collapses the possibilities into one outcome and the reality that comes with it. If you go with, "This dog never listens to me. She'll never get it right," the defeated energy that comes with that thought permeates the space, and the dog feels it.

The exact mechanism by which this happens is not clear, but you can test it yourself. I simply think of it as working with energy.

Here is an example: Have you ever left your house in the morning in the most fabulous mood? You slept well, the morning routine in your household went smoothly, the sun was shining, you did not encounter any traffic on the way to work, and your favorite song even came on the radio. You arrive at the office and head to the conference room for your first meeting, where the boss is chewing out one of your coworkers. BAM! You just walked into a wall of negativity and your good mood rapidly diminishes.

We are deeply influenced by the energy of those around us, and, in turn, we are also energy influencers. This leaves us with a choice. At the cusp of thinking, you can fold into familiar self-defeating thoughts, or you can keep yourself in the realm of possibility by not indulging in the same old negativity. Others may collapse their possibilities into blind alleys and dark corners, but we have a choice not to go down that rabbit hole.

Are you meant to never have a thought again? No, that would be impossible. The trick is to not let your thoughts conk out into dead ends. In fact, in superposition, since many thoughts are simultaneously true, you can hold multiple ideas at the same time. We tend to like straight answers, clear decisions, and predictable outcomes, but to rest in the field of potentiality requires that we get comfortable with ambiguity and paradox. I was not sure about this myself at first, but I quickly learned that there is the potential for anything to happen from this place, including a dramatic behavior change in myself, which brought about dramatic changes in the animal beings I was working with. As I furthered my studies, the field of potentiality became increasingly easier to access.

HOW TO ACCESS THE FIELD OF POTENTIALITY

Your relationship with your pup can be one of the most rewarding experiences in your life, but it can also be challenging. It will ask of you things that no other relationship will ask, and it will give in ways that no other relationship can. For it to be successful, you will need to do some inner work to stay positive, solutions-oriented, and open to new possibilities. This work may not seem so related to getting your dog to stop peeing indoors or sit when you ask them to, but trust me—your attitude and your energy are critical, foundational aspects of a successful life with your dog.

One of the most common challenges I encounter in the people I work with is repetitive negative thinking (RNT). It keeps them from understanding their dog's perspective and from accessing the field of potentiality where solutions to the problems are available. RNT commonly takes the form of worrying about the future or ruminating on the past. We all do it at one time or another, as our brains have a negativity bias built into them that has served us well evolutionarily. After all, if we are scanning for trouble, when we occasionally encounter it, we will have a better chance of managing it. But in our modern world, most of us do not live on the knife's edge of survival. So instead of staying sharp to listen for predators, our brain finds something else to fixate on, something not life-or-death, like the fact that your dog does not listen to you.

If what you are putting out into the world is negativity, guess what you are going to get back? Problems, disasters, emergencies, and things to complain about. And the more you amplify these things, the more you seem to find. But, as author Pam Grout says in her book *E-Squared,* "Every "wrong" thing, which in reality is nothing but a foolhardy judgment, has a flip side. Lack is the flip side of abundance. Sickness is the flip side of health. Both ideas exist at the same time. Both are true. By choosing to see one aspect, the other equally likely aspect is hidden."

Sounds a lot like our puppy in the box with the gunpowder, right? If both positive and negative thoughts exist at the same time until we choose one, how do we choose the positive one when we are programmed to seek negativity? And how do we do it without slipping into denial and just pretending there is not an issue to be addressed? Where do we go to access this abundant energy, find creative solutions to our problems, and access the field of infinite potentiality?

As Deepak Chopra says, "You must find the place inside yourself where nothing is impossible." Once you see your own potential as limitless, you will see your dog for who they are, and you will be able to work with them on anything. To do this, you need to do what you do with your dog: practice. Practice getting to know your mind and learning how it can work *for* you and not *against* you. Practice reframing your thoughts and the events that happen to you. Practice being less judgmental and taking a different perspective on things. Exercise your muscles of resilience and curiosity.

Below are some of the more popular practices or ways you can develop this all-important self-awareness. Your goal is to find something that helps you step back a little so you can observe yourself. Something that leads you through a process of becoming aware of how your mind works and how your feelings and emotions influence you. As you spend time looking at yourself this way, you begin to notice how your behavior affects others. You start to see habits and patterns that interfere with your relationships—human and canine. Over time, and sometimes with the help of a coach or therapist, you slowly become more open, less reactive, and more curious about the world and how others experience it, as well as how you can change it for the better.

I want to acknowledge upfront that this personal development work is often not easy. It requires commitment, discipline, and sometimes help from others. But it is necessary work that will reward you with satisfying, mature relationships with the dogs— and people—in your life, if you are willing to put in the effort.

Meditation. Meditation continues to grow in popularity as evidence builds that it can help with many things, including reducing anxiety and stress, managing anger, lowering blood pressure, and more. There are many styles of meditation out there, including well-known mindfulness practices like Mindfulness-Based Stress Reduction. Perhaps you are drawn to a concentration practice or one based on a more relaxed, open awareness. Maybe you like chanting, contemplative prayer, listening to music, or reading a passage and reflecting on it. You might like sitting in stillness or walking mindfully through the woods. Experiment with different types until you find one that works for you, one that brings spiritual insight, new ideas, or unique solutions for perplexing issues. Discovering your inner ability to reach a peaceful, contemplative state will bring you clarity both in your life and in working with your dog.

Shamanic/Spiritual Practices. As I opened within this chapter, one of our fundamental challenges is we have forgotten our place in the natural world. Many shamanic and spiritual practices can help us reconnect on that level. You may want to explore Native American or other Earth-based spiritualities that have ways of connecting and communing with animals. Read about other traditions. Attend ceremonies. Open your mind to other ways of seeing and being in the world. Experiencing the beauty of what others have to offer is also a beautiful way to reinforce or come to appreciate your own faith and beliefs even more.

Spend time observing nature. If a nature-based spirituality is not for you, you can still benefit from spending quiet time in nature. Take a walk in the woods. Sit beside a lake or a river. Put your feet in the ocean. Step up to a tree and touch its bark. Hang up a bird feeder and get to know your local avian inhabitants. Step outside at night and look up at the stars. Try to imagine how the world would appear if you were one of these astounding beings, even just for a brief moment. Simply stepping out your door can prove to you that time outside helps shift your state of mind, but in case you want proof, there is an abundance of research available that links time in nature to better physical and mental health. And when we feel better and calmer, we are likely to be able to see possibilities we would not have otherwise.

Find your happy place. One of the best ways to shake loose from your typical ways of thinking is to lose yourself in something you are passionate about. Find something you love—and do it! But do it with a twist: pay attention to how you behave and how you feel when you do it. Just zoning out and removing responsibility or accountability is not going to change anything in your life. But activities such as running, hiking, knitting, crafting, painting, writing, cleaning, mowing the lawn, playing an instrument, and yes, even video gaming—if you bring attention and awareness to how they influence your ability to let go of negative obstacles causing you mental congestion—all these activities and more can help you gain access to an infinite world of new possibilities.

Personally, I find relaxation in the realm of Dungeons and Dragons, listening to music, playing instruments, resting in a hammock, and hanging out in a field with my canine brothers and sisters. I spend ample amounts of time with my family exploring the bountiful beauty of what nature has to offer. It helps me to step out of the more challenging parts of my life and allows me the space to release my mind and refresh my ability to cope with everyday issues and demands. It gives me a way to relax and experience the truths in life so I can then shift back into the provider role, facing trials and tribulations of society with a different perspective.

Talk to a coach or therapist. Sometimes our patterns or habits are so deeply ingrained we fail to recognize them, or we have some significant past trauma to process, and we need a little help. Luckily, there are many people out there that possess a special gift of guidance and are trained to help you make sense of your past and find your way to a happier and more peaceful future.

If you are dealing with a difficult issue with your dog, it can be easy to think there are no good options left. But trust me when I say the solution is there inside you, often in plain sight. My challenge to you is to find your way to the realm of possibilities and commit yourself to your goal. Do not entertain failure. Find the feeling of success, reach into the field of potentiality, and let it show you what to do. Anything is possible, and you owe it to your relationship with your dog to shift the dynamic to allow for them to thrive. You are far more powerful in this realm than you know, and with practice, you will see how dramatically you can change the world for you and your furry friend.

These practices are not just a suggestion. They are integral to my philosophy and they are an important part of my work with clients and of what I teach in workshops. Finding ways to open your mind, build self-awareness, and become conscious of your canine companion's particular needs are the foundation for any further work to come. In fact, when people commit to developing themselves in this way, positive results with their dog are almost guaranteed. I am not saying the path will be easy— when addressing the psychological nature of any being, including canines—you may run into resistance behaviors. You may open doors that bring forth repressed traumas, unchallenged desires, and hidden potentials. Staying open-minded and patient will give

you the greatest possibility for success.

The gifts of a dog are timeless and essential. I believe there is nothing in a human's life that is as profound as the dedication of a dog. They provide happiness when comfort is needed, security without hesitation, and love that can fill the emptiest of hearts."

—David J. Kurlander

3
Which Dog is Right for You?

One of the most frequent questions I get asked is, "What kind of dog is right for me and my family?" I love this question, because it indicates a person realizes the importance of choosing a compatible companion—one that will match their household and become a valued member of the pack. There are many obvious factors that go into the decision of which dog to welcome into your family. Typically, people think about the size of the dog, the size of their home, the cost, and the amount of time they have to commit to caring for them. Sometimes they look for a dog for a specific purpose, like hunting, protection, or service. But often people ignore even these basic considerations and choose a dog because they like the way it looks, as if it is an accessory or an object indicating social status.

All of these criteria are missing one thing: the dog's point of view. While we do not want to leave out the human's needs, it is important to think about how we would answer this question from the dog's perspective. To do this we need a basic knowledge of breeds—from pure to mixed to designer—as well as an appreciation for the role of genetics in behavior and an understanding of the "nature versus nurture" conversation. Then we can revisit the question at hand to find a good match.

THE RANDOMNESS—AND HELPFULNESS—OF BREED CATEGORIES

Humans like to categorize things in an effort to understand them. In the United States, the American Kennel Club (AKC) is the organization that sets the standard for breeds, providing a detailed checklist of what qualifies a dog as a particular breed. Each breed then has its own national club that helps manage the breed standard and often helps rescue dogs of that breed. The AKC currently recognizes 195 breeds (out of up to 450 worldwide), which it lumps into seven groups: sporting, hound, working, terrier, toy, herding, and non-sporting.

While all this is helpful for organizing our way of perceiving the canine world so we can care for breeds properly and keep our furry friends healthy, there is a way of looking at breeds that can help us better understand why they behave the way they do. First, let's go back a bit to our domestic canine's closest wild cousins, the wolf. Wolves have two key characteristics that help them survive and thrive: hunting and protecting. The very survival of the pack depends on each wolf playing their part and taking the needs of the whole into consideration over the needs of the individual.

In hunting for food, they use a range of techniques, including tracking, herding, pointing, retrieving, and flushing. The pack often hunts together and communicates in various ways as they do so. Wolf pups have a predisposition to the hunting drive— you can observe them stalking a blowing leaf or leaping on a cricket at a very young age (innate behavior we also witness in domesticated canines). The pups learn additional skills through what looks to us like play, as well as through discipline from older wolves, especially their mama.

When it comes to protection, wolves will do whatever they need to do to defend the pack—from disciplining each other and the pups to working together to ward off predators. Wolves will mark territory to ward off other predators and use intimidating body language when they feel threatened. They are also masters of eluding danger. Avoidance, or running from impending threats, is often the best way to avoid unnecessary injury and is their main line of defense.

Every dog, domestic and wild, is born with a purpose. While all of them can typically hunt and protect to some degree, individuals have natural talents, so some will be better pointers or herders, etc. When humans began to domesticate dogs, we selected ones that had particular traits we found useful. Communities living near water favored dogs that could swim and catch waterfowl, like the Portuguese water dog, who has been helping fishermen bring in their nets for hundreds of years. People tending sheep in the mountains looked for dogs that could assist with bringing the sheep in for the night and alert the shepherd when a predator was nearby.

As the millennia passed and people continued to select dogs for particular characteristics, we slowly changed the genetic profiles of these animals. A few hundred years ago, we started refining breeds in earnest, eventually arriving at the diversity of breeds we have today.

We could say then that a breed is simply a group of dogs bred to do a certain task; a group whose genes have been manipulated by humans over thousands of years of selective breeding for a specific purpose. All breeds fall into two primary categories based on that purpose: hunting and protection. Within those categories, you will find dogs with specialized behaviors because we have bred them to have a particularly refined sense of smell or hearing, or drive.

For example, the Labrador's webbed feet and double coat make them great swimmers, even in cold water, where they can retrieve birds for their human hunter. A Bracco Italiano, on the other hand, has a natural ability to hold back and point in the hunt, a characteristic that has been retained and elaborated upon through selective breeding. A Bloodhound can track a scent in a way almost no other breed can; its sense of smell and drive making it an unflagging search and rescue dog.

While our modern breeds exhibit different characteristics based on how we shaped their evolution, they all retain some mixture of the survival skills of their ancestors. We may have played with the focus of that drive, but that drive is always there in some form. We have enhanced dogs to do certain things well, and, regardless of whether we ask them to live in an apartment in the city, in a house in the suburbs, or on a farm, we need to honor that genetic heritage and help them live out their soul-driven purpose.

A FRUSTRATED HUNTER

Many hunting breeds have an affable and easygoing personality that has helped them find their way into our homes and families, like Labrador retrievers, Golden retrievers, Springer spaniels, Irish setters, and more. Most of these dogs will fit right into family life and live quite happily with their human companions. But sometimes a dog acts out, and one of the most common causes of the problem is that a dog has a particularly strong drive or internal genetic purpose that is not being satisfied.

Several years ago, a woman called me to say her Lab was "murdering" all the birds and the wildlife in her fenced-in yard. She was convinced that there was something psychologically wrong with her dog—that he was malicious and evil and needed to be fixed. She had called several professional dog trainers who told her that the dog had a "screw loose" and needed to be euthanized.

Luckily, her veterinarian called me before allowing her to euthanize the dog. With just one visit, the dog made a 180-degree turnaround. How did that happen? It is not because I have magical skills. I simply taught him and his family how to appreciate, embrace, and manage his natural instincts. We set up a few routines that simulated hunting using feathers and wings. The dog was immediately responsive and satisfied, their person was thrilled with the change, and the pack went on to live a long and harmonious life together.

All dogs, to one degree or another, are hunters. A frustrated hunter is not "broken" and does not require "fixing." They are only doing what they were designed to do. And by neglecting to provide opportunities for them to fulfill their purpose, they are destined to be frustrated and act out in some way.

WHAT GENES CAN TELL US

You may be thinking, "My Bodhi is no hunter—she was lounging on the couch one day when two raccoons wandered into the house through her doggie door and helped themselves to food off our kitchen counter. She did not even lift her head off the pillow!" It could certainly be the case that your dog does not show any signs of the hunting instinct, but that does not mean it is not there. Given the right circumstances, your dog may very well exhibit behaviors similar to her distant wolf cousins. The moment the comforts of home are no longer accessible, or the structural dynamics change, rest assured their survival instincts will kick into gear.

Most people are looking for a dog that is "pet quality." They want a docile, easy-to-manage animal who will not demand too much and will not cause any trouble. I do not think of dogs as pets. In fact, I avoid using the term. Companions, family members, furry familiars—yes. But calling them pets sets up a divide that diminishes the dog's individual experience and their importance. When thinking about innate behaviors, I prefer instead to refer to dogs as "high-drive" or "low-drive." A high-drive dog is one who exhibits strong hunting or protecting behaviors. Low-drive dogs exhibit little to none of these behaviors, which is what people are looking for when they think "family pet."

How do we know if a dog is high- or low-drive? Part of it is genetics. If I take two very strong hunting breeds and breed them, the puppies have a greater likelihood of being high-drive hunters. Breeders watch early on for signs of drive in puppies. I have done it too when looking for a hunting dog for myself or a client. If there is a litter of eight puppies and six of them are pointing at feathers and leaves at eight weeks old, we know we have some potential hunters. They may all have different temperaments and personalities, but they are high-drive dogs born to hunt. What about the other two who do not show any interest in hunting? In my experience, even with a low-drive dog, the nature of the hunter is still there, and with a proper understanding of their needs, and appropriate training, it can be brought out.

How much of this drive is determined by genes and how much is influenced by breeding two high-drive dogs? While it is common practice for breeders to breed for drive, and it makes logical sense, Dr. Christos Suriano, a neuroscientist at Princeton University, says we are still very far from understanding how genes affect drive, temperament, and personality. "Genetic networks are incredibly complicated. Since the dog genome was sequenced in 2005, we have been able to identify the genes responsible for things like coat color and eye color. But the genetic toolkit required for complex behaviors like the hunting instinct is still being worked out. It makes sense that these instincts are passed down through genes, but the science is just not there yet. Because we are limited in what we know about genetics, breeders need to be careful, as breeding to increase one particular trait could have unintended genetic consequences on other traits."

The other role genetics plays in breed management is screening for diseases and inherited weaknesses. If breeding is not managed well, genetic problems can emerge. Over time, if there is not a large enough gene pool to draw from to correct the problem, the breed will reach a point of no return. One of my favorite breeds, the Bracco Italiano, is prone to a genetic mutation that causes kidney failure at around four years old. This is one of the most ancient breeds, dating back to the second century BC. It is as popular in Italy as Labradors are in the United States. With too much breeding taking place outside of the Bracco Italiano Club's infrastructure, the breed is coming perilously close to crossing the line. If it does, the breed will eventually perish. Currently, the Bracco Italiano Health Foundation is working to stabilize the genetics of this breed so we do not lose this, over 2,000-year-old line of canines.

Genetic profiling is also important for America's favorite dog, Labrador retrievers. Some Lab breeders breed for high-drive, looking to produce good hunting dogs. Others are aiming for low-drive, trying to decrease the hunting instinct to either make for a more laid-back animal around the house or for a seeing-eye dog where it is important the dog does not bolt after the first squirrel to cross their path. Other backyard breeders do not even think about drive or health and are simply breeding cute puppies for quick cash.

Regardless of the intention, there is a tremendous amount of unregulated breeding happening with Labs, and along with it a marked increase in a genetic neuromuscular disorder called Exercise Induced Collapse (EIC). A dog with EIC can lose muscle strength in their back legs, lose coordination, and possibly even collapse after a short burst of strenuous exercise (even as little as 5 minutes). There are many good breeders out there who will neuter a dog they could stud for a lot of money when they find out that the dog is carrying a genetic problem like EIC. Others will invest time and tremendous expense to breed out the genetic defect. These breeders put the love of the breed and respect for these special companions over greed.

There is often a divide in how the public views dog breeders. Those who love "shelter dogs," by which they typically mean mixed breeds, often feel that with so many dogs needing homes, we should not breed dogs that are so expensive. While it is true there are many wonderful dogs in shelters (we will talk about mixed breeds later in this chapter), I believe that breeders play an important role in maintaining the ongoing health of our canine companions and preserving a breed's purpose. It is a responsibility I believe we took on thousands of years ago when we started domesticating canines.

When we bring a dog into our home, we are expanding our family. They become an integral part of our life—playmates for our children, protectors of our homes, exercise partners on our daily run, and cuddle buddies on movie night. Having removed them from their natural environment and having shaped them to fit our needs, we owe it to these animal beings to care for them in the best way possible. That means maintaining their genetic health so they can live long and happy lives with us.

I have heard many tragic stories of both purebred and mixed breed dogs who die prematurely from preventable diseases. By paying more attention to their genetic health, we can make it more likely that we get to enjoy each other's company for a good long time. This is not to say that I do not think there is no room for improvement in holding breeders accountable for ethical practices—it is my philosophy that we can always do better by each other and our furry friends. We should strive to continue to improve the system for the benefit of all.

UNDERSTANDING TEMPERAMENT & PERSONALITY

While genes play an important role in how a dog behaves, genes are not destiny. Much like identical twins have exactly the same DNA but wind up being very different people, each dog has a distinct personality and sees the world in their own way. They are their own unique individuals, with a particular temperament and personality, and understanding them on this level is crucial giving them a happy life as well as addressing any behavioral issues.

I think of temperament as the scaffolding of ourselves. It is deeply, if not exclusively, influenced by genetics—it is the fundamental nature of who we are. It is eternal, immutable, and unchangeable. Layered on top of that is our personality, which includes our temperament but is also connected to something ineffable—I call it spirit. It is the thing that makes you uniquely you, and it wants to be the fullest and purest expression of itself throughout your life. It has a fundamental expression but can also be shaped and changed.

Let us think about it in terms of you for a minute. Your parents would confirm that you came out of the womb with a certain temperament, a particular way of being; some moms would say they could sense your temperament even in the womb. As a newborn, you may have been easily agitated or preternaturally calm. You may have liked bright objects or shown no interest in them whatsoever. However you were, you seemed to have arrived that way—and if you had siblings, even an identical twin, you were distinctly, fundamentally different from them.

It works in exactly the same way with dogs. Each pup comes into this world with a particular temperament. They may be driven to hunt or protect. They may be fearful or fearless. They may be calm or rambunctious. Upon that scaffold, their own particular personality and spirit begin to emerge. One fearful dog may be hypervigilant and avoidant while another might be an aggressive barker. One peaceful dog may be reserved and independent while another might need to be on your lap all the time. A dog can be social, quiet, goofy, affectionate, smart, easy-going, observant, oblivious, or any number of other attributes. Whatever their particular combination of characteristics, the best thing we can do for the dogs we bring into our life is to provide them with the opportunity to be who they are and to thrive.

Take for example Labrador retrievers Bridget and Stella. From the beginning, Bridget showed virtually no desire for the hunt. She prefers to spend her days on the couch where she is strategically placed to get as many belly rubs as possible. If she sees a feather, she either runs the other way or hesitantly approaches it and starts playing with it. When she plays with her siblings, she will perform perfect points and stealthy stalking techniques, hiding around corners before pouncing on her unsuspecting sister, but generally speaking she has a passive, gentle personality.

Then there is her sister Stella. Born of the same litter and almost identical in appearance, Stella is a hunter to the core. She is independent, confident, and would stop a train if she could. While Bridget is getting her snuggles in on the couch, Stella is lurking around the yard for her next pursuit. I like to call this the pursuit of happiness. While both dogs exhibit hunting abilities when they play, only one has the high-drive to act on it and wants to play the role of provider for the pack. These two dogs have very different temperaments and personalities as well as different purposes to fulfill.

My American bulldog Riley was another great example of the complexity of temperament and personality. Riley loved the chase. He would run after nearly anything that moved, given the chance. He was born that way. But his personality was such that if he caught something, he would only love it to death! He caught a rabbit once and laid down and immediately started licking it as if to groom it. So, while the hunt is part of him, his sweet personality means he would not hurt a fly, even if he went all out to catch it.

But even under this sweet personality, he had strong defensive instincts that protected me on numerous occasions. One day we were walking in Pelham Bay Park in the Bronx and an extremely agitated man approached me yelling profanities and flailing his arms aggressively toward me. Riley instantly turned from a sweet-natured dog into the fiercest guard dog I had ever seen. It was as if someone flipped a switch in him. He did not approach the man at all; he simply bore his pearly white teeth and held his ground between me and the belligerent man. He growled deeply and thrust his head to the side with sharp, intermittent barks, communicating clearly, "Back off!" The man avoided us completely, still yelling and making a scene as he went off down the street.

Why did Riley react this way? It can seem confusing that a dog with such a sweet personality would act this way, but this is a great example of an internal natural instinct. Because he never exhibited a proclivity toward protective behavior when he was young, I did not encourage it. But underneath the goofy, loving hunter was this protective temperament. Like humans, dogs are complex beings and we need to spend the time getting to know them.

IT IS ABOUT NATURE *AND* NURTURE

Knowing your dog's temperament and personality can help you answer a very important question: "What does my dog expect from me?" Dogs, like people, are shaped by their circumstances. Getting to know our canine companions for who they are can give us insight into how to nurture that uniqueness so they can live a fulfilling life.

Let's go back to you for a minute. As you grew up, your unique personality emerged. If you were lucky enough, you had a parent who recognized the singular expression of your spirit and helped nurture you to your full expression as a human being. In many ways, that is what my mom did for me in nurturing and supporting my love of animals as I grew up. Most of us, however, have parents who had their own idea about who their kids should be. These parents, often with the best of intentions, make their children conform to a way of being and behaving that is not their own. This is not to blame anyone—parenting is a demanding job, and we all do the best we can.

In addition to your parents shaping your personality, you were also influenced by circumstances and interactions with others, such as teachers, extended family, coaches, and religious communities. With each encounter, you subtly adapted yourself to meet the varying expectations put on you. If you strayed too far from your innate temperament and unique spirit in this process of growing up, you might eventually feel like you are living someone else's life. Since your unique and unchangeable temperament determines how you process your life experiences, if you fail to listen to your inner self, you may find you are behaving in ways that are harmful and destructive to yourself or others. This is a tough position to be in, but the good news is that underneath it all, you remain uniquely you and can get back to a more authentic expression of yourself with some work and commitment.

Dogs are subject to the same rules—their personality and behavior is strongly influenced by the world around them. A study published in 2019 by Evan MacLean, Noah Synder-Mackler, and colleagues looked at the heritability of 14 traits in dogs, including things like excitability, energy, touch sensitivity, separation problems, fear, and aggression. The study found that behaviors are indeed highly heritable and even identified 131 places in a dog's DNA associated with differences in behavior. But their conclusion was that only about 15% of a dog's personality can be explained by DNA.

Snyder-Mackler explained, "It is important to keep in mind that we looked at breed averages for behavior. We're not at a point yet where we can look at an individual's genome and predict behavior. Environment and training still has a very, very strong effect." In other words, depending on how a dog is treated, one type of behavior could come to dominate over another.

Your dog will come with their own temperament and personality. How you nurture them will not change their fundamental makeup, but it can change their behavior, which can make all the difference in whether your dog is happy and well-integrated into your pack. Take, for example, a pup with a fearful temperament who tends to be aggressive when he is afraid. In a conversation I had on my podcast with neuroscientist Dr. Christos Suriano, he confirmed, "The environment in which this pup is raised will be a huge factor in their resilience. An animal with particularly aggressive genes, if raised in the right context, might yield totally different results." My experience bears this out.

I worked with a Springer spaniel called Gunner who was particularly dominant. Having a dominant nature in the dog world is not a problem—dominant dogs have the ability to lead and provide for the fellow canines in their pack. But in a family, a dominant dog can be the source of a lot of distress if their energy is not properly directed. Gunner was a brilliant dog who wanted to be in control of his environment. His family tried a number of training methods, but Gunner found his way around them all. With treat-based training, if you did not give him his treat quickly enough, he would snap at your leg or grab your clothing. Using a prong collar to force his compliance (a method I do not endorse) only made him assert himself even more as he tried to defend himself.

Gunner's family could not find any more trainers who would work with them, and several recommended euthanizing him. Luckily, the family veterinarian passed along my name before agreeing to end Gunner's life. When I met Gunner, I saw a dog with impressive natural instincts, so I asked if I could take him out as a hunting partner for a day. Gunner shined like summer sun! With a little direction, he was pointing, flushing, and retrieving without hesitation. I saw zero evidence of aggression or possessive behaviors in the field. When I returned Gunner to his family that night, he jumped up on me and licked my face as if in thanks for such a special day. In the end, Gunner's family decided to share him with an extended family member who had just taken up pheasant hunting. From that day on, Gunner never exhibited aggressive behaviors again.

Whether a dog is aggressive, protective, passive, or loving, we should not try to smother or change them. This is where most "dog training" goes wrong. Instead, we should look for ways to direct their natural way of being into behaviors that are more acceptable in our world. Training to make a dog behave in a particular way is unnatural. It asks a dog to suppress their innate temperament or personality, and much like us, if they do that for too long, they will often begin to behave in ways that are truly problematic.

What I aim to do is find a way to let them flourish as they are, to help them live in a world that is so foreign to their wild sensibilities—one of cars whizzing down the street and cats sleeping on the couch and human children pulling on their tail. I advocate for patience over punishment. If you are willing to work with your dog in this way, then you can nurture them to use their nature differently, no matter what their predisposition. You are always nurturing something, and if you pay attention, you can provide them a socially acceptable way to be themselves. Line up your nurture with their nature and everyone will be satisfied.

This understanding of working with an individual's personality explains why there is no one-size-fits-all way of dealing with behavior issues, and why your role as a nurturer will be dependent on the individual needs of your dog. While you may know something about a breed's general temperament, and that can be a good place to start, you will always need to take the individual dog into consideration.

THE CASE FOR AND AGAINST MIXED BREEDS

I often get asked about mixed breeds, which are frequently available in shelters or through animal rescues. Let me start by saying that I have brought many mixed breeds into my home, and they have been wonderful family members. I also work closely with a number of shelters, helping them with behavioral rehabilitation to increase a dog's chances of being adopted. And I sometimes assist with integrating mixed-breed dogs into their new home. According to the American Society for the Prevention of Cruelty to Animals (ASPCA), there are more than 3 million dogs brought to shelters each year, and about 75% of them are mixed breeds. That is a lot of dogs that need homes, love, and care, and that is exactly what they all should get.

When thinking about adopting a dog, there are several challenges to evaluating whether they will be a good fit for your family. For starters, it is very difficult and sometimes impossible, to tell which breeds make up a mixed breed dog based on looks. After decades of experience with more than 150,000 dogs, I have some skill at being able to guess which breeds make up a mix, but this is not a skill the average person possesses. Today you can get a DNA profile of your pup that will tell you their unique parentage. This can give you a place to start to look for temperament, but even if they look like one of the dogs in their ancestry, they could act like another. Even puppies from the same litter can display different traits. Perhaps one will act more like a Doberman while another brays like a Beagle. And that dog that looks so much like a Labrador retriever may be 25% German shepherd—and there is no guarantee the dog will act as either of those breeds. In fact, the mixture can compound behaviors and be very difficult to comprehend.

Having no knowledge of the genetic makeup of a dog leaves you at a loss in assessing their temperament for two important reasons. First, you do not have a starting point for knowing the general breed traits. Is their lineage hunting, herding, or protecting? Second, even if you can make an educated guess about a dog's temperament, there is also their personality to consider. While personality is individual, some of it is also passed down through the genetic lineage. Not knowing the disposition of a dog's parents leaves us again in the dark. The best you can do is to watch for your dog's particular spirit to emerge when you bring them into your home and then do what you can to fulfill their needs.

One additional challenge to adopting a shelter dog is that it is difficult to get an accurate take on their temperament and personality in such an unnatural setting. While shelters are necessary to give dogs (and other animals) a second chance in life, dogs typically behave quite differently in these spaces. After adoption, a dog's true nature will often emerge about three to six months after they settle into their new environment and drop their guard in the safety and permanence of the new pack. It is only then you might discover that behind that relaxed, sweet, mellow puppy is a highly predatorial canine who was just waiting to be freed. I get many calls from people who say, "They were so quiet for the first few months, and then they went crazy!"

Statistics indicate that up to 20% of dogs are returned to the shelter within six months of adoption. But if you have already fallen in love with your new family member, a sudden behavior change is not a deal-breaker if you are willing to do the work to meet their needs. Most people I encounter expected a docile dog who would just integrate seamlessly into their life, if they even thought about what they were hoping for at all. They did not expect to have to do so much work to figure out their pup. If they are willing to stick with it, I tell people to watch and observe. You will soon see signs that the dog really needs to run or that they need to find things—there will always be a breed trait that stands out the most. If you approach the relationship with dedication, understanding, and love, you will have a much better chance of successfully integrating your pup into your family.

Another important factor to be aware of with mixed breeds is the dog's health. Reputable breeders take painstaking care to ensure their dogs have the genetic makeup to live a long and healthy life. Unethical, unauthorized backyard breeders do not give any thought to the dog's health and longevity. They are aiming to produce cute puppies for a quick sale and, as a result, mixed-breed dogs often suffer from undiagnosed or unknown health issues that emerge when the dog is a few years old.

When you adopt a dog, you fall in love. I have met many families who are devastated by the loss of their dog at the age of just four or five from illnesses or diseases that are screened out by responsible breeders but that are not monitored with mixed breeds. Does this mean you should not adopt a mixed breed? Definitely not! I am not a purist, but I do think you should go into the decision with your eyes open. I encourage everyone who adopts to purchase a genetic profile that includes a panel of common disorders. This way if you know the dog will be genetically prone to something like kidney problems, you can take steps to prevent it.

I know there are many dogs in shelters needing homes, and I think those willing to take on elderly or sick dogs are true heroes.

Before I had children, I adopted many dogs who I knew would not live very long. But now that I have kids, I no longer do that, as it is a sorrow I do not want to put my children through. No one likes to lose a companion. This is an individual decision, but if someone is looking for a dog to be with them or their family for many years to come, I encourage them to look into a purebred dog from a reputable breeder or, if they are adopting a mixed breed, get a genetic test done first to know what might be ahead.

THE CHALLENGES OF "DESIGNER" BREEDS

In some sense, you could say that all breeds are "designer" breeds—we humans have been both actively and subtly enhancing dogs' natural instincts for our benefit since we first forged this relationship. However, in recent years, there is a disturbing trend happening where some breeders are ignoring the dogs' best interests and are thinking only of what people want.

We are forgetting about their genetic and evolutionary purpose and manipulating them for our desires and our needs.

The English bulldog is an example of a dog that has been bred for no other reason than people like the way it looks. These dogs often have "Brachycephalic Obstructive Airway Syndrome" (BOAS) and cannot breathe well. They cannot run without doing damage to themselves. They may have chronic ear, eye, and skin infections, and other health issues that require repeated care and attention. Like several other breeds, the puppies' heads are typically too large to pass through the birth canal, so births can only happen via cesarean sections. If humans suddenly disappeared and could not assist these dogs in surviving, the breed would likely go extinct.

I know there are many loving and dedicated people committed to this breed, and I am friends with some of them. But I have a larger question about what we are doing with breeds like this— and with other dogs we are breeding with the intention they play the role of an accessory in our life. Is this a kindness to the dog? Does breeding them as house pets respect their unique evolutionary heritage? I do not think so. I have worked with many English bulldogs and have loved every one of them, but the breed as a whole leaves me with an unsettled feeling. I cannot help but think we are doing an injustice to the canine species.

To breed a dog to be no more than a "house pet" takes them further and further from their origins and crosses an ethical line. Dogs have a genetic purpose, and we cannot breed that fully out of them. Even with all its aesthetic changes, English bulldogs still want to hunt. But to be saddled in a body that does not allow them to do that is not a kindness. When a dog is welcomed into a home with the expectation that they are going to sit on the couch and watch TV all day and not demand much attention other than the occasional treat, it is a recipe for trouble. People typically blame the breeder or the dog, when instead they should be asking how they can help these amazing beings live a fulfilling life.

Currently, the most popular designer breeds are those crossed with the Poodle. From Labradoodles (Labrador retriever/Poodle) to Goldendoodles (Golden retriever/Poodle) to Yorkiepoos (Yorkshire terrier/Poodle), there has been a rush to breed many different dogs with Poodles in an attempt to make a hypoallergenic family pet. While they do shed less, there is no scientific proof that Poodles are hypoallergenic. In fact, a study published in the American Journal of Rhinology & Allergy in 2011 found that homes with hypoallergenic dogs had the same level of dog allergens as homes with non-hypoallergenic dogs.

The first Labradoodle was "created" by the Royal Guide Dog Association of Australia in response to the request of a blind woman who wanted a guide dog that her husband would not be allergic to. Knowing that Poodles shed less, the head breeder, Wally Conron, tried to train more than 30 Standard Poodles to be guide dogs. But none of them could meet the rigorous standards. He decided to try crossing a Poodle with one of their best Labrador retrievers and subsequently could not find anyone interested in taking the pups. According to Conron, he approached the association's public relations team for some help finding homes for these dogs, and the "Labradoodle" brand was born.

You might think Conron is proud of what he created, but it is just the opposite. "I opened a Pandora's box, that is what I did. I released a Frankenstein," he said, some years later. "So many people are just breeding for the money. So many of these dogs have physical problems, and a lot of them are just crazy. All these backyard breeders have jumped on the bandwagon, and they are crossing any kind of dog with a poodle. They are selling them for more than a purebred is worth and they are not going into the backgrounds of the parents of the dogs. There are so many poodle crosses having fits, problems with their eyes, hips, and elbows, and a lot have epilepsy. There are a few ethical breeders, but very, very few."

I am with Conron on this one. I get many calls about "oodle" breeds. Often it is because people expected a docile family dog and are surprised to find out they have a dog who is acting aggressively and possessively around their food or stalking the family cat. If you are breeding two dogs with massive hunting drives, as is the case with the Labrador retriever and Poodle (which is a French pointer, an extremely intelligent and dominant dog), it makes sense that you have a good chance of winding up with a high-drive dog who wants to hunt.

Protecting their food and chasing small animals are normal behaviors for dogs, especially high-drive dogs. Their "aggressive" behavior is not personal. They do not hate you and they do not hate the family cat—they are just acting out their instincts. Once you understand that, you can chart a course of action to meet their expectations so you can all live together harmoniously. If you have welcomed a hunting dog into your high-rise in Manhattan, it is going to require significant effort to get your dog to stop lunging at pigeons, which is why it is important to consider both your needs and the dog's needs up front and perhaps pass on whatever "oodle" breed is the latest trend, no matter how cute they are.

CHOOSING THE RIGHT DOG FOR YOUR PACK

I hope you can see by now how critical it is to find the right match when welcoming a dog into your home and your family—both for your happiness and for the dog's. Dogs have a purpose. They have expectations for their life, just like you. When those expectations are not met, they might exhibit fear, anxiety, or aggression. Since they cannot interview or screen us as potential pack mates, it is up to us to take their needs into account. This means you do not go with just what *you* want—you also consider their needs and be honest about how you can fulfill them. The following questions can help you get started:

- What can you offer?
- What is your lifestyle like?
- How much time do you have to commit to a dog?

- What is the current makeup of your family/pack and how will the dog fit in?

- What types of activities do you want to do with your dog?

- How much indoor space do you have to accommodate a dog?

- How much access do you have to parks, trails, or hunting fields?

Take some time to reflect on these questions and see if you can distill the answers into a sentence that reads a bit like the top line of a dating profile! As you answer these questions, you will start to bring some clarity to your situation and what you can offer. You may even want to write it down like this:

- I am an active person who likes to be outside and am looking for a dog to go running with me each morning.

- I live alone and am looking for a quiet companion to keep me company and to go on evening walks with me.

- We want a gentle and playful dog to be a playmate for our kids.
- We have a huge vegetable garden and want a dog to help keep the groundhogs off our property.

What if you realize you are a busy professional who travels a lot and can only dedicate 10 minutes a day to a dog? Then you might have to come to terms with the fact that a dog is not right for your lifestyle. In this case, you are putting the needs of the dog over your desire, a noble and generous act. And it does not mean you cannot find other ways to have a dog in your life—look to spend time with other people's dogs or volunteer with a rescue so you can still experience these amazing beings.

Once you have a clear sense of your situation, you can begin to research breeds. Of course you can use the internet to learn about the characteristics of various breeds, but I encourage you to talk to breeders and speak to those who live with the breeds that interest you. Put yourself in the shoes of the drive and temperament of each breed, and be honest about whether or not you can meet their needs.

Consider these questions:

- What does the dog need?
- Does this dog have a high-drive or low-drive predatory nature?
- What is their physical stamina like?
- How much outdoor space do they need to be themselves? Would a small city park do, or will the dog need more open space to run and explore?
- What activities will satisfy them physically, mentally, and emotionally?
- What is their inherent "job"? Is their breed typically hunters, herders, or protectors?

If you decide to go with a mixed breed or a shelter dog, know that you may not get answers to many of these questions.

Sometimes shelter staff can make a good guess, but just know that you will have to pay extra attention and be ready for any kind of behavior to reveal itself over time.

No matter which dog you welcome into your pack, it is important to model behavior and start training the moment you take the leash. Even if the dog seems to have a perfect temperament, you have to establish yourself as the provider and lay the rules for what is expected in their new environment. If you do this, you are well on your way to a pleasurable and memorable life with your new family member.

To be pack is to elevate beyond the simple meaning of family. As a tree needs the soil to support its roots so it can stand, a dog needs a pack for love and support so they can thrive. Without the pack, the individual will not feel whole."

—David J. Kurlander

4

Pack is Everything

Canines are pack animals. You might think that we humans are too—after all, we live in families and have a tendency to cohabitate. But we can also go off on our own and live as hermits, building shelter and growing or foraging for food by ourselves. Depending on our personality, we may even prefer this lifestyle to a lively and sometimes chaotic social life.

But going it alone is not an option for canines. If a "lone wolf" splits off from a pack for one reason or another, they will not last long. A canine's very survival depends on being part of a group and on knowing their place within it. Our domestic dogs carry in their genes an expectation for a certain structure, but when we welcome them into our home, they are joining an unusual pack that evolution did not necessarily prime them for.

As providers for these animal beings, it is our responsibility to understand what our canine pack member is expecting and then to communicate clearly with them in a way that they will understand. You set the tone for your pack. The dogs in your family rely on you to be a leader—to give them direction about what to do and how to behave in this strange world of cars, couches, and kibble.

I would venture to say that 99% of having a harmonious pack is dependent on understanding structure and communication. If your dog appears anxious or aggressive, looking to understand their behavior through the lens of pack structure will give you new insights into how to work with them. It will also help you understand why many traditional training approaches either work only under certain circumstances or do not work at all. And it will give you the path to providing what your pack truly needs— safety and stability—which is the most effective way to address behavior problems.

UNDERSTANDING PACK STRUCTURE

In Western society, we have a hierarchical way of looking at the world. We see things as having a pyramidal structure, where those at the top have most of the power and the rest of us are either submissive and defer to them or are aggressively trying to climb the pyramid to topple and surpass those at the peak. Our governments follow this model, where the people are represented by an ever-decreasing number of representatives as we move up the pyramid until we get to the top, where there is one person "in charge." We also follow and admire this model in business, where we have come to idolize CEOs who receive extraordinary levels of compensation and garner cult-like celebrity status.

But does winning an election or having a financially successful business make you a good leader? By all accounts, no. Would these folks be where they are now without everyone else underneath them working hard to support the vision? Most certainly not. Does their status guarantee that they are qualified to lead? That is a big no. Yet we persist with this myth of the benevolent, self-made leader.

This understanding of leadership is a human, ego-based perspective, one we have had for millennia. When we began to study wolves and wild dogs, we projected this benevolent leader model onto them, and in the process missed some key observations about the true structure of a pack. It is not wrong to say that there are pack leaders; it is inaccurate, however, to place outsized value on one position over another. It is not like a pyramid—it is more like a distributed leadership model where pack members are capable of filling in various roles depending on what is needed. From "top" to "bottom," there is an orientation to doing what needs to be done to protect the integrity of the pack.

THE MYTH OF THE ALPHA POSITION

One of the main purposes of a pack is to encourage the young to grow up to be strong providers for the community. To protect the pack and to hunt for food requires strength and aggression, and this behavior is encouraged in pups. As we discussed in the previous chapter, not all pups will exhibit these traits—it depends on their personality. But those who have a tendency toward this type of behavior are often seen as potential challengers for the canine equivalent of the CEO—the alpha dog.

One of the most persistent misunderstandings about pack structure is this idea that there is an almighty benevolent alpha (or an alpha pair) who is in charge and will hold that position as long as they can fight off any contenders. It is true that one wolf will typically be in the position of "leading" a pack of 20 to 30 or more wolves. It is also true that these tend to be the wolves that are the strongest-willed and most regal. But they are not in charge of everything in pack life. They are *responsible* for food, safety, and keeping order among the pack, but they do not do it alone. I call these leaders "providers" instead of alphas, and I use the word alpha to refer to a mentality.

The alpha mentality is a constellation of particular character traits that lend themselves to being *a* leader (not *the* leader) in a pack. This mentality is one of great intelligence, independence, and stubbornness. A canine with an alpha mentality knows when and how to appropriately communicate with other pack members, including when and when not to use aggression. Many members of a pack, male and female, will have some level of an alpha mentality. Some are born with this temperament, and mamma wolves nurture this behavior, knowing it is good for the pack.

Because the safety of the entire group is at stake if the top provider cannot do their job, pack members will often test the provider to make sure they are strong enough to continue performing their duties. What we see as aggressive challenges to the top dog are actually just pack members asking the question,

"Hey, you still got this?" If a provider fails the test, any number of pack members will be ready to step in and assume the role. It is like having a number of backups in case one hard drive fails or spare light bulbs at the ready for the next time one winks out. This constant checking and the capacity for a quick succession is important to the integrity of the pack. It maintains social order and ensures that there is a stable environment for continuing to raise the young.

Having many pack members with an alpha mentality also means that if a provider is away from the pack to hunt or scout there will not be a vacuum in leadership. While the provider is gone, others can step in as necessary. This distributed leadership approach is also beneficial on the hunt, where there is not a single leader calling all the shots. The hunt is a sophisticated event with many roles, including flusher, pointer, scout, bait, and ambush team. Through wordless communication, they share the responsibility and decision-making process to ensure success.

One way to visualize the structure of a pack with multiple dogs with an alpha mentality is as a collection of totem poles or ladders. If you assume that the top position on the totem pole is the most dominant (a popular misunderstanding about the iconography of totem poles, but one that works for our analogy), then in any given situation there is a structure that the pack would recognize. But there is not just one leader for all situations. A pack is like a collection of totem poles and the position of "top dog" can be held by a different pack member in different circumstances. For example, a mamma is a provider for a micro-pack within the larger pack.

THE IMPORTANCE OF MAMMAS

While the fictional "alpha" has gotten an outsized amount of attention from the world, the role of the mamma canine is often overlooked and underrated. Unlike males, females can fill every role in a pack, from provider to protector to parent. Mammas operate on two primary levels—as members of all roles in the macro pack as well as providers for their own micro pack (her litter of pups), meaning that a breeding female carries the most responsibility of any pack member.

Typically, the top providing male will mate with one female, though there are documented accounts of multiple mating pairs in a pack. The biological father is not typically involved in raising the pups, at least not in a direct way. Once she has her litter, mamma must feed and protect them not only from the dangers of the wild, but from members of her own pack that might be aggressive toward the new pups. Without her finesse and skill, the whole pack would collapse.

To keep an eye on the present and future of the pack simultaneously, a mamma canine must have a very strong alpha mentality. She must be clear, decisive, strong, and fearless. This does not mean she is overly aggressive—it is typically the opposite. She is noble, tenacious, steadfast, and commanding.

She will not fight unless there is a big structural battle. And then, look out!

Another reason mamma canines have what I think of as the most important role in the pack is because they are responsible for raising the pack's future providers. Mamma will do whatever it takes to keep them fed, and she will raise them to have the strongest alpha mentality they can have, based on their personality. If she happens to raise a future male or female top provider, then they will have gotten to that place through a combination of nature (their genetic inheritance) and nurture (the guidance of their mamma). No matter how dominant a male gets, it is mamma who gets him there.

With their outsized influence, if I were pressed to say who was the true leader of the pack, I would pick the breeding female. A female can assume every single role in the pack, but a male cannot. Beyond the hunting, protecting, and internal peacekeeping in the pack that both males and females can do, the females are in charge of the future of the pack. She of course will show deference to the top male, but I believe it is with an eye toward building up his alpha mentality. She will submit willingly for the safety of all, not because he is more dominant or capable than her.

Because of their smart and tenacious character, if a client wishes to get a dog for protection, I will always recommend a female. With that motherly instinct, when they shift into protection mode, often even without any training, they can be ten times more fearless and ferocious than a male. They are also independent thinkers who can make judgment calls on their own, which can be a good or bad trait depending on your needs.

This general impulse is also why I recommend males as hunting dogs over females. Both will hunt with fierce dedication, but in my experience, the males are easier to train, that is once you break through their initial hardheaded stubbornness. These are generalizations, of course. I have trained amazing male dogs as protectors and female dogs as hunters. As always, our canine friends are individuals, and we must take into account their temperaments and personalities. But as with breed characteristics, considering their genetic inheritance can give us some good insight.

WHAT'S MINE IS...MINE? POSSESSIVE BEHAVIOR

From the beginning, mammas must strike an important balance with their pups. They have to encourage the alpha mentality, but they also have to ensure that mentality is tempered enough so each pup understands the interdependent nature of the pack. The moment they begin nursing, the pups with a more dominant personality will growl and push other pups off the nipple. Mamma will respond to them with vocalizations and growls and by simply picking them up and rearranging them. In doing so, she makes sure they know that she is the one in charge of distributing available resources. She says, "This is mine, and I provide it to you under these circumstances." She does it in a way that stops the pup's behavior in the moment but does not suppress them developmentally.

This scenario may sound familiar to you. I often have clients tell me their dog does the same thing over and over again (barking at squirrels, jumping on guests, rooting through the trash, chewing the furniture) despite being told no in any number of forceful or coercive ways. People often accuse their dog of being stupid. Your dog is not stupid, nor are they willfully ignoring you. They are simply acting as their nature drives them to act, testing the limits of the fences like the dinosaurs in Jurassic Park. We will talk about this more in the chapter on training, but stopping a dog's nature by suppressing it, which is how many training techniques work, is like trying to stop a river from flowing. The water will go somewhere, so either you can choose to redirect it repeatedly, like mamma does, or it will find a way to be expressed. If you find a way to fulfill your dog's purpose, chances are good that they will be satisfied and fit seamlessly into the pack.

As pups grow older, they learn to both hunt and eat on their own or with the pack, and food possessive behavior will remain one of the primary means of understanding pack structure. As they go through their days, if they happen to catch a rabbit, lizard, snake, mouse, or squirrel, they may enjoy the meal on their own or bring it back to some pups. Either way, they will continue to communicate with each other through possessive behavior to show who is the more aggressive and dominant. When there is a group kill, generally speaking, the dominant pack members tend to eat first, warning the others off with what may seem like vicious snarls and attacks. But I have seen it happen over and over again while the dominant wolves are eating that a pup trots right up to the kill and starts eating alongside them without ever getting corrected or sent away. The dominant ones understand that the pup needs to eat too; that the future of the pack is dependent on everyone getting enough. It is a lesson they have been learning since day one.

Possessive behavior is a means of communicating an understanding of structure in a pack. In my pack, I can take anything away from my Black Labrador Cinder, but the other dogs in the pack cannot. He clearly holds a higher position over the other dogs, and they respect that. Yet, he perceives me as his superior and will not show his teeth, growl, or nip at me. I have observed similar behavior with wolves in captivity. At feeding time, the dominant ones are the first to explore the offerings. The less dominant ones wait their turn. If they do not want to wait and decide to approach the food, the higher-ranking wolves show their teeth, growl, and raise their hackles. If the lesser ranking wolf persists, the higher ranking might give a dramatic corrective display that includes a bark and bite. From outside the pack, we might view this as aggressive brutality, but if we look at it from the inside, it is just normal canine communication. It is a beautiful way to maintain the structure they so depend on to ensure the survival of the pack.

Food is not the only way dogs find their place in a pack structure. They also use aggression to possess their space. In the wild, that looks like possessing a den or an area where an individual is resting. Or it could be a mamma protecting her pups from a particularly aggressive older member of her own pack as a way to demonstrate who is in charge of those pups. At home, it would look like your dog growling at you when you go near their kennel or when you tried to move them off the couch or the bed. A growl is their natural response—it is their normal way of trying to communicate that there is an imbalance in the pack structure. Because they do not see you as the leader, they see themselves as equal to or above you in the pack structure at that moment and feel they can claim possession of the object or area.

I often tell clients that this kind of problem is like a branch on a tree. The roots of the tree are the inherent temperament and personality of the dog, which is mostly genetic. The trunk of the tree is the emotional tone of the dog, while the branches represent the categories of habits and conditioned responses that a dog develops over the course of their life. The leaves are the problematic behaviors and actions that grow out of these habits. (We will return to this illustration in Chapter 7 where we will explore how to deal with common problems.) To solve these behavior issues, people often try to cut off the branches by using aggression, bribing them with treats, or capitulating and letting them stay on the couch "this one time." But like the river that will just flow elsewhere, the branch will just sprout again. In fact, three more branches may sprout in its place. Alternatively, you can get to the root of the problem and build a strong pack structure through routine and leadership, which will create new habits and, ultimately, new actions. Going back to the source gives you a controlled and supportive way to address any behavior issues.

A FEW MORE OBSERVATIONS FROM PACK LIFE

Dogs are social animals, but a pack is introverted. Canines are incredibly social creatures. They hunt, play, eat, and sleep together. The group supersedes the individual, and they instinctively know they cannot survive without each other. Take grooming as an example. I have never seen a wolf or a dog that can fully clean their own ears. They need another pack member to clean them. In my own pack, I can tell if my hound dog has an ear infection because my Labrador will spend more time than usual licking the hound's ears. They need each other. And while pack members may have strong social bonds, those bonds do not extend beyond the pack. I have never seen a wolf or a coyote leave its pack for a play date with a canine from another pack. And no matter how much I worked with wolves in captivity, I always needed to remember that I was not pack. As humans, we are much more social with other groups of humans outside of our primary group, but it is helpful to keep in mind that this is not necessarily our canine family member's natural inclination.

Packs coexist with other animals around them. Wild canines are instinctively aware of the balance of life and how to maintain it. A deer could walk by a wolf and if the circumstances are not right for a hunt, or that wolf just ate and does not need more, they will let that deer walk by undisturbed. And a pack will never decimate an entire deer or elk population in a given area—it would go against the long-term survival of the pack. With a natural instinct for balance, wolves and coyotes keep other animal populations in check. They will often cull the weakest, which ultimately strengthens the other animal's pack or herd and controls overpopulation, which supports the health of the whole ecosystem.

Submission is internal, fear is external. Inside a pack, a canine will show signs of submission to other pack members with a stronger alpha mentality, especially toward the primary pack provider. They may wag their tail, lower their head, expose their belly, lick the other canine's mouth, make themselves smaller, or flatten their ears—whatever they need to do to appear non-threatening. These gestures indicate their understanding of their position. They are a form of respect and comfort that helps maintain the safety and wellness of the pack structure.

Outside of a pack structure, this behavior indicates fear and confusion, not submission. I see many dogs in shelters exhibit this kind of behavior—wagging their tail, lowering their head, exposing their belly—and people will often comment, "Oh, look! That is great, they are a submissive dog." Unfortunately, this is not an accurate conclusion. Dogs do not submit to anything outside their pack. So, while the behaviors may look the same on the outside, they do not mean the same thing—much in the way we humans might smile either out of happiness or fear. In the case of a dog appearing submissive to a stranger, they are actually afraid and confused. They are not submitting because they see that person as a leader and want to join their pack.

This is why there are so many stories of someone adopting a shelter dog that seemed so docile and submissive at first but a few weeks later attacked the neighbor. In the shelter, that dog was confused and lost. Once inside a pack (at home with you), they could come out of their shell and let their true nature as a dominant dog come out. This is why we should not coddle dogs, even the ones who act submissive. When bringing a dog into your pack, immediately set the boundaries of structure by developing healthy communication and you will subvert these behaviors before they even arise. They must know that you are calling the shots. And if they turn out to be a more dominant, aggressive dog, that is okay as long as you are guiding that personality to express itself in acceptable ways. If you establish yourself as the one who provides for their food, safety, and well-being, then they will take their cues from you in all circumstances.

CREATING STRUCTURE IN YOUR PACK

There is nothing more exciting than welcoming a dog into your family. How can you take the knowledge of how a wild pack works and use it to integrate a canine companion into your home as seamlessly as possible?

First, you must realize that a dog's understanding of human culture is extremely limited. When they arrive at your home, they will immediately assess the situation to determine who is part of the pack and who is in charge. They want to know who is included: is the baby part of the pack? The teenager? The cat? Where are the boundaries?

Their understanding of "pack" is very limited and typically includes only those who live together and share food. While I might consider my childhood friend part of my family/pack, a dog will not see it that way. In fact, I have such a friend who stops by maybe once a month, and my dogs are always happy to see him. But if he were to approach one of my dogs and try to take away their bone, my dog would rightfully growl to warn him off. This is known as "resource guarding." It is a way of demonstrating possession to members outside of the pack—you are guarding the resources of your pack. While my friend gets a growl, my 2-year-old could walk right up to the dog and, without incident, simply remove the bone from my dog's mouth. Why? Because my child is pack and has a role in the day-to-day life of my dog. Since my friend is not around every day, he is not part of the pack in my dog's mind.

A new arrival in your home will also want to know who the providers are—where is food and protection coming from? They are completely at your mercy, and the best thing you can do is work to establish a clear routine, which will give them a sense of safety. If you do not fulfill the role of provider, they will either feel obligated to step up and fill it, or they will feel rejected and become fearful. Their uncertainty over who is in charge is the source of a significant number of behavioral problems.

So, is your new pup looking for "the alpha"? No. Remember, there is no "alpha," as such. There are providers, and there can be multiple providers in a pack. Often there are one or two people in a position of authority, followed by older children who have more responsibility than the younger ones because of experience and maturity. The older ones are always looking to educate, protect, and provide for the next generation. The survival and safety of the pack is the responsibility of all, not just of a single top dog.

In addition to developing the routines that establish you as a provider, you will want to help your dog fulfill their purpose. Your dog wants to participate. All pack members play a role, and your dog wants to play one, too. In some way, shape, or form, you need to find a way to meet their expectations and give them an active role in the pack. Just like people, they need a purpose to feel fulfilled. What is your dog's purpose? That is for you to figure out with them based on their breed, temperament, and personality. Do they want to herd, hunt, nurture, or protect? Finding creative ways to allow them to do their part will go a long way to helping them feel satisfied. It will also cut off many behavior problems at the root.

So how exactly do you establish this structure and come to understand what role your dog can play in your family? Communicating with your canine family member is key.

COMMUNICATION IS KEY

While we love the dogs in our life, they are dogs, and we are humans. When it comes to communicating, there is a thick brick wall between us. We cannot knock that wall down because then we would be dog to dog or human to human, and that cannot happen. But we can drill holes in the wall—we can talk, connect emotionally, compromise, and make an effort at understanding how our furry family member sees the world. We will never communicate with them as clearly as they communicate with each other, but that does not mean we should not try, because, without communication, we have nothing. Or worse, we have a messy, uncomfortable, and frustrating situation.

This is just as true with human-to-human relationships as it is about human-to-canine ones. When a dog joins your family, they are coming to you with a certain understanding of pack structure and the knowledge of how to communicate within that. But what is acceptable in a wild canine pack is not always acceptable in human society, and since we are bringing them into our world, we have a certain obligation to learn how best to communicate with them. In a very real sense, you could call this a relationship book, and the foundation of any good relationship is communication.

I will occasionally get a call from someone who wants to stop their dog from doing something like jumping onto the bed. In order to work with that person around this behavior issue, I will begin by explaining the importance of structure and communication. More than once, I have had people stop me and say something like, "That is great, but it is not relevant to me. I just want them to stay off my bed! Tell me what I can do to keep them off. Food? A shock collar? Put a big object on the bed?

My response to this is that we are not a good match to work together. This person is not interested in hearing what I have to say, let alone what their dog has to say. They are impatient and have already stopped listening, and listening is a critical part of communication. In addition, any relationship based on punishment or shame hurts a dog's psyche. It may solve the immediate issue, but it will not solve the deeper misunderstanding of structure that the dog is trying to puzzle out. If a person does not want to look at things in a different way, then they are not likely to take the time to see the world from their dog's perspective and learn how best to communicate with them.

When we welcome a puppy into our family straight from their mamma, we are taking them from the family structure that thousands of years of evolution prepared them for and bringing them into one that is completely foreign to them. Remember the analogy to the roommate? Your new puppy was just taken from the pack where he understood everything that was going on and put into a pack where no one speaks their language. Imagine how stressful that is!

When we attempt to communicate with our new pack member, it shows a sense of care and concern—it gives us a way to lay down the structure for them, helping them make sense of their new surroundings. When we attempt to communicate clearly, with an understanding of their way of seeing the world, they cannot help but respond with an eagerness to please, grateful that someone cares enough to speak their language.

"SPEAK, FIDO, SPEAK!"

This may seem so obvious that it is not worth stating, but it is important to point out that dogs do not use human language. Even though we know this, we still talk to them with the expectation they will understand. People often say things to me like, "I told her a thousand times not to jump up on people when they come to visit!" Verbal communication is our most conspicuous and perhaps our most dominant means of communicating with each other as humans, and because we often (even unconsciously) assume the role of the superior species, we talk to dogs and assume they should understand. Because they have been attuning themselves to us for thousands of years now, it can seem they do sometimes get what we are saying. After all, we ask them to sit and they sit. But are they sitting in response to our request, or to get the treat hidden in your hand? More likely, it is the latter.

Dogs communicate primarily through emotions and body language. Vocalization—making growls, grunts, whines, or barks—is part of the way they communicate with each other too, but it is not primary. When a provider returns to the pack with a kill, they will communicate with vocalizations who gets to eat first by growling at those who need to wait. Wolves will communicate to and about potential threats or enact a role call via growls and howls. From the beginning, when pups are first born, mamma will communicate with them through low growls and noises as she grooms them, and she builds the framework and values of pack structure as she manages who nurses when.

In my experience, the longer a puppy can stay with their mamma, the better adjusted they will be to their human family in the long run, especially hunting dogs. My dog Kuno, a Braque du Bourbonnais pointer, was with his mamma and his sister until 8 months old, and I have never once had a behavior issue with him. I took him off the leash and he was immediately responsive to me. I have seen similar results with other dogs who stayed with their litter longer. My hypothesis is they have more time to learn the value of the pack's structure and that makes the communication easier on our end once they join our families.

Either way, you have to establish structure through natural communication first. Once that is established, dogs have the desire to respond to you. This relationship fosters a different kind of loyalty than a food reward. If you are relying on their desire for food in order to get their cooperation, what happens when they are not hungry, or they do not like that particular food any

longer? If they rely on you as the provider, they settle into their

position in the pack, and then it is simply a matter of consistency

and repetition to get them to do things like sit, stay, or lay down.

In addition to listening to us speak to them, dogs often speak

back to us. To understand what they are saying, we need to read

some of their non-verbal cues. For example, they may paw at you

as if they are trying to get your attention. Or they might bark or

make sounds as they seem to stretch forward and lower the front

part of themselves to the floor in a kind of "downward dog" yoga

position known as a "play bow." These are ways of

communicating that they are in a playful and non-threatening

mood. I use a simple communication scale when trying to

understand canine communications, especially around aggressive

behaviors. The scale goes from 1 to 100, and anything below 50

is considered a pre-escalated behavior. Playful vocalizations are

pre-escalated and are approaching 50, but at some point, if the barking or growling passes a tipping point, behavior can escalate very quickly, often shooting to 100 in a second.

We will look at how to use this scale when working with behavior in the next chapter. For now, it is important to know that this threshold is different for each dog, meaning you are going to need to take the time to get to know the temperament and personality of the dog you are working with to understand what they are saying when they speak to you. First, let us explore dogs' primary means of communication: emotion.

IT IS TIME TO GET EMOTIONAL

Dogs, like humans, are emotional beings. We both love, we both hate, we both feel fear, and we both desire to live a life where our needs are satisfied. While our capacity to feel emotions is similar, how we express or communicate them is different. Dogs live more in the moment, navigating the world from a primarily emotional lens, whereas we add layers of thinking and cognition on top of our emotions and sometimes they are not as easily accessible to us. As the ones who have brought dogs to live in our world, it is our responsibility to spend a little more time in the emotional field so we can better read them and respond to their needs.

Dogs are incredibly attuned to emotion, especially within a pack. Because they need each other to survive, and because they need to be quiet when they hunt, they learn to read body language very accurately. Unlike humans, who can just tell the butcher which cut of meat we want, canines must get quiet and communicate, often over a distance, with a level of nuance and intuition that defies our ability—though in the days before grocery stores when we too hunted for our food, I imagine our capacity to do this matched that of our canine companions.

We may not be as good at sensing or expressing emotion as we used to be, but it is still important to our communication. Many people think emotions are messy and are to be avoided. But without emotion, you have no motivation, no personality. Emotions are like the tires on a car—they make us go. Without emotions, we have no connection to the world. We cannot hate or love or feel joy or sorrow.

This does not mean we let our emotions run unchecked. It seems like the whole point of being a grown-up is to gain some level of control over our emotions and maintain a balance with them so they enhance but do not rule our life. We have to embrace our emotions as well as set boundaries on where they lead us. And we must know when to let those boundaries go, like when a beloved animal friend dies, and we feel the tremendous sorrow of the loss. Yet even then, we must work to not let the boundary go so completely that we throw ourselves off a bridge in despair.

Emotion also gives us the capacity to do superhuman things, like lifting something extremely heavy or running long distances in an emergency. Emotions like frustration and annoyance can also be great motivators that get us to take action. Often these emotions are what drives someone to contact me when their tolerance of their dog's behavior reaches a breaking point. While you do not want to suppress emotion, you want to find ways to have balance and control, to some degree.

Dogs swim in this emotional sea. It is their primary way of interfacing with the world. You could say they are more in sync with that natural state of being than we are. They are experts at reading the room for its emotional tone and responding accordingly, without thought. When they experience extreme emotion in the wild, they move through it and shake it off—literally. After a moment of fear or confusion or joy, it passes through, and they find themselves in the next moment. Their emotion is felt by the rest of the pack, who responds accordingly if something needs to be addressed. As a whole, the emotional tone of the pack helps regulate each individual canine—when one goes outside the normal emotional tenor, the power of the pack eventually brings them back to an equilibrium.

What happens with many dogs living in a human world is that their emotions go unacknowledged and unheard. They try to communicate to us that they are unhappy, perhaps with a look or a certain way of holding their ears or vocalizing. If we ignore this, their efforts to communicate will only get louder, graduating to what we commonly think of as behavior problems. They have now become what we might call "overemotional" in a human. And since they rely on the pack to regulate them back to baseline, if their human companion is ignoring them, they have no recourse except to get "louder." The longer a dog goes unheard, the harder it becomes to correct the behavior, which is why learning to work this way with your dog from the beginning is always the best. As the saying goes, an ounce of prevention is worth a pound of cure.

Regardless of how long a dog has gone unheard, you can still make inroads. The potential to change the relationship is right there below the surface, but it will take some changes on your part. Seek out help. Learn the difference between behavior and training (coming up in our next two chapters), open your heart to your canine instead of being angry at them for simply trying to communicate. Your dog is counting on you. Let go of the human thought processes that so desperately seek an explanation or a fix for everything and start actually breathing in the cool air or feeling the warmth of the sunlight that lays upon your skin. Free your mind and simply feel. Shut off the incessant questions and simply be. When you take time to access this fundamental, emotional state of being, you will be much closer to understanding your canine companion than you would be otherwise.

MEETING IN THE MIDDLE

Another important relationship skill to master is compromise. This topic comes up a lot during my behavior consultations with families, who, even without a dog in the mix, are always looking for a balance among their members. No one member can take, take, take without the other members getting disgruntled or angry. While many people make too much of "their dog," treating them with excessive attention or accommodation, an equal number of people see the family dog as just a beast, no more than an accessory or decoration in their life, like the pool in the back yard or the fish in the tank.

But dogs do not see "human" and "canine." Their pack is the people they are with. Their home is the family, not four walls and furniture they are not supposed to chew. In a wild pack, a canine will witness dramatic battles of top-ranking pack members over a fresh kill, or a mamma protecting her pups from an aggressive pack member. There is a balance between what is necessary for the betterment of the whole with the understanding of individual boundaries. When one member crosses a boundary, they are reminded of their place and must accept that compromise. They typically do, but if they do not, and the dynamic continues to be fraught, that member may split off from the pack.

Since splitting from your pack is not an option for your dog—they need us as a provider of food, safety, and love—it becomes our job to find a way to let our canine family members be the individuals they are while also maintaining the harmony of our pack. We cannot expect our furry friends to be housebroken, not chew on anything, walk on a leash, and do silly tricks (e.g., sit, stay, and lay down)—all things they do not do in a wild environment—without giving them something in return. We will not be able to meet their expectations 100%, but we must find a compromise that meets their needs and lets them feel that they play a role in the survival of the pack.

In my family, there is me and my wife, our kids, and three dogs. There are a lot of needs to manage in our pack, and, of course, no one gets 100% of what they want. Sometimes we each have to take less than what we would like in order to maintain the good of the whole. For example, let us say one person does not love socializing in groups but the other family member loves big gatherings. Where is there room for compromise? How can you get creative so that both parties feel like they are seen and heard? Maybe you put a time limit on how long you are at the event, or you take separate cars so one person can stay longer, or you agree to accept every other invitation. These kinds of compromises allow you to honor each other. They acknowledge that you love each other despite, or sometimes even because of, your differences. And it honors the importance of the family structure.

With dogs, it is the same. If I am a vegan, I may need to compromise and provide my dog with the meat-based nutrients they biologically need. If my dog is a natural hunter and wants to chase squirrels in Central Park, I will need to find a way to let them experience the thrill of hunting by using antlers, wings, or retrieving bumpers (floating decoys), even if we never go on an actual hunt. If my dog loves to come up on the bed but I am worried about ticks, I might want to buy them a soft and cozy bed of their own and spend some time sitting on the floor with them where they can be close to me (and then go do a tick check afterward, of course). These kinds of compromises will help ensure the integrity of the family and make your canine family member feel safe and secure.

A LITTLE EFFORT GOES A LONG WAY

Tapping into the field of emotions and figuring out how to make creative compromises will go a long way to resolving behavior issues with your dog. Why? Because effort is everything. I cannot say this nearly enough to the families I work with. Make an effort—any effort, no matter how small—and you will see change. When you show care and concern for another's well-being, even if you cannot meet all their needs, they appreciate it.

What does effort look like? If you have made it this far in the book, then there is a good chance you realize there is something to fix in your relationship with the dog(s) in your life. You are already making an effort, and just a shift in your perspective can begin to make a change.

You can try implementing the lessons in this book yourself, or you can find a dog trainer or dog behaviorist to work with. There are many different styles out there and finding someone you resonate with will make it much more likely that you will keep trying. If you are not comfortable with their approach or methods, then you will not make the effort necessary to help your dog. I strongly encourage you to do the work yourself. It has become fashionable to send dogs away to "doggie boot camp" for somebody else to fix the problem. People spend thousands of dollars and the dog returns home and falls back into the same behavior patterns because the problem is not just with the dog— it is with the pack dynamic. And you cannot change the pack dynamic without doing the work yourself.

There's an American-born spiritual teacher named Adyashanti who has this equation: time + attention = intimacy. I love this. Time is a gift. Attention is a gift. When we give these gifts, we get something back—a deep, bonded relationship of respect and kindness. You can buy or bribe your dog with treats or toys, but it will not develop the same depth of rapport that giving them your time and attention will. It is the ultimate expression of effort.

Jamie is a cocker spaniel I had the pleasure to work with who was a perfect example of this principle. This special little boy had a sweet nature but with dominant tendencies that got him into trouble. Born deaf and blind, he had a series of families that did not make the effort to understand his special personality and unique needs. That is until he finally found Brenda. Brenda fell in love with Jamie and was willing to make extraordinary efforts to understand how to work with him. As soon as Brenda started to make an effort, Jamie responded. Brenda has learned what Jamie needs and Jamie has learned what is expected of him. It is an equal exchange, and with this support, Jamie has been able to lead a happy, healthy life. He has tapped into his own potential and is one of the sweetest dogs I know.

I have seen many difficult situations, and it is natural to feel defeated and lost at times. But it is up to you to change this dynamic and find a way for your pack to live in harmony. Your dog knows how to give love. They can feel the pain of rejection and fear. They are aware of your state of mind and are communicating with you every moment of every day. Do not give up on them, because they are not giving up on you. There is a way out for 99% of the situations I see. (There is the rare occasion when a dog has truly become too wild and dominant or has become too ill to fit easily into a typical family pack, but these occasions are truly few and far between.) With an understanding of structure and communication, you are now ready to learn the difference between working with behavior and dog training and to develop some routines to put these principles into action.

Behavior is internal and natural. It is what guilds the outcome of events. It is what nature intended for us to make a special impact in this world and influence reality as we know it to be. Behavior is our identity and defines our reactions.

—David J. Kurlander

5
Behavior: A Natural Approach

Pulling on the leash. Peeing in the house. Rooting through the trash. Growling, whining, and barking at inappropriate times. Interrupting you when you are talking to someone or trying to focus on a task. Dominantly mounting animals, furniture, or people (commonly referred to as "humping"). The list of behavior issues that people have with their dogs is seemingly endless.

Like human psychology, dog psychology and behavior is complex. After decades of working with these amazing beings, I still encounter new scenarios and variations on themes all the time. No dog, person, environment, or set of experiences is the same from one situation to another. In the same way that every human child acts out differently, every dog will have its own personal way of responding to the world. Because every scenario is unique, it would be impossible for me to provide one-size-fits-all routines or easy solutions to working with behavior.

What I can do is offer you some general principles and illustrate them with some examples—but be aware that this is not out-of-the-box technology. You may not want to launch into these routines on your own. Instead, the information in this chapter will give you a solid understanding of what it means to work with behavior so you know what you are looking for when hiring an animal behaviorist.

WHY IS MY DOG BEHAVING THIS WAY?

When working with behavior, the first place to begin is with this deceptively simple question: *Why is this dog behaving in this particular way?* While we ultimately hope to answer the question, of course, simply asking the question is an important way to reframe your relationship with your dog. You could just have an idea of the behavior you want and then set about finding the best means to coerce your dog into behaving that way. This is what training is all about. (We will talk about the difference between behavior and training later in this chapter.)

However, looking to get to the root of the problem requires us to take the dog's perspective into account over our own ideas of what we want. It is a critical shift of thinking that puts you in a place where you can honor their experience and access the field of potentiality, where there are solutions you could never imagine. Of course, you still hope to get what you want in the end—a well-behaved dog—but this approach is about understanding them rather than just applying standard routines and hoping they will work. With this change of perspective, you can start to refine your question to something like: why does my dog feel so uncomfortable, out of place, or entitled to act out in this way?

I almost always begin my quest to answer this question by asking clients about the medical history of the dog. Dogs are stoic creatures when it comes to pain. They do not emote like we do, and sometimes the signs of physical problems will be behavioral. Perhaps your dog's breed is prone to kidney failure, thyroid issues, or certain types of cancer. Or maybe they have a toothache, an ear infection, digestive issues, or worms. They could be going blind or deaf, or have injured themselves somehow. If a dog's behavior issues have come on suddenly, I always ask my clients to take them for a thorough checkup.

I worked with one family whose dog had suddenly gotten aggressive around food. She did not understand why the dog was hungry all the time—she was feeding them twice a day, as she always had. It turns out the dog had an intestinal parasite that resulted in severe diarrhea. So while they were eating more than ever, they were not getting enough nutrition because it was all being eliminated too soon. The poor dog was simply starving. Your dog may be eating their own or another dog's poop or dirt because they are nutritionally deficient. They may be incessantly licking their paw because they have an allergy. Ruling out a physical issue can help save a lot of time and energy and get your pack back in balance sooner rather than later.

I once had a call about a dog who started whining all the time when in the house. When he was outside, he was fine—but as soon as he came in and laid down, he whined. The vet diagnosed him with anxiety, so the person contacted me to work with that behavior. But in our initial assessment, we discovered the dog had a spine injury that caused him pain when he laid down and relaxed. When he was up and moving it did not hurt, so the whining disappeared. The whining behavior disappeared quickly once we got him the right medical treatment.

If your dog's problem is not stemming from physical pain or discomfort, there are endless psychological reasons they may be acting as they are. No matter what their particular scenario, and while the variety and creativity of ways with which dogs "act out" is impressive, there is essentially one root cause, and that is an imbalance in their relationship with you.

PACK STRUCTURE IS THE FOUNDATION

As we discussed in the last chapter, for your dog, the pack is home. What they need from their home is simple: they need a clear understanding that they are safe and will be provided for, and an opportunity to contribute to the pack in some way as well. When you confidently communicate to your furry family members, "I have got this, and I have got you," they can relax, be themselves, and play a role in the pack that makes sense to them. Once they know they are part of a well-cared-for pack, they will be more than happy to follow your lead. If they get the slightest whiff that there is a gap in leadership in the family, they perceive the pack may be at risk, so they start trying to accommodate for that in ways that we experience as problematic. Their attempt to find an equilibrium is read by us as a behavioral issue when it is a natural response to an unstable situation.

If we expect dogs to coexist with us and be "good," we must realize that we are asking them to live in an environment foreign to the one that their evolutionary lineage prepared them for. While it is impressive how well they have adapted and attuned themselves to us, they still have no innate understanding of our world. They do not think in terms of "good" behavior and "bad" behavior. Perhaps your dog has a strong inner drive to chase things. They do not know the difference between the squirrel at the bird feeder or the car driving by your house—they see something moving, and something deep in them stirs to the hunt. In fact, sometimes the messages from us can be confusing: "You want me to chase the deer out of the garden but not the neighbor's cat? How am I to know the difference unless you tell me?!"

Dogs need guidance to help make sense of our world, and that leadership needs to come from you and other family members. As I said in the last chapter, I am not a fan of sending dogs away to "doggie boot camp." Those programs can work for training dogs to do things like hunt or search and rescue, although you have to have a foundation of healthy behavior for any training to work. For behavioral issues, YOU need to build a relationship with your dog. I can easily get your dog to behave well in my home with my dogs, but if the underlying structural issues in your home have not been addressed—if they still do not respect you, do not know their place in the pack structure, or do not feel safe and secure around you—then when they come home, the problems will inevitably resurface.

The primary goal of working with behavior is to convey to your dog that you provide them with security, food, protection, and love of the pack. For canines, the pack is where everything exists. And when they get all their needs met there, they do not want to leave. If they see you as their provider, they will check in with you and defer to you before doing anything. Here is a story that illustrates this in a dramatic way.

I was out bird hunting one day with my dog Malachi, a Bracco Italiano. We were in an open pasture on the edge of the forest. It was a picture-perfect day with a steady wind and blue skies. I sent him in search of a bird, and off he went. Within moments, he was on steady point. Suddenly, not far from where he was headed, a coyote, who must have been resting, was startled by Malachi and stood up from the long grass. Then another one raised its head. And another. There were maybe 10 of them. Malachi was a significant distance from me at this point, headed right toward the coyotes. But then he caught their scent and stopped in his tracks, pulled his head up, and turned to look to me for guidance. This is one of the most driven bird dogs I have ever worked with, and he just stopped his pursuit and turned to me as if to say, "What do you want me to do?"

I whistled for him, and he started to trot back toward me. But as he did, the coyotes started to advance toward him. So I stopped him and told him to wait. I ran toward him so that now it was not one versus ten, but two versus ten, which meant the coyotes would be much less likely to get aggressive. When I got to Malachi, he came right to heel, and we walked toward the pack a few steps. This confused them and they scattered into the woods before we reversed direction and headed back to the car.

Malachi did not look to me for guidance because we had spent hours and hours training for this kind of scenario. He did not do it because he expected a food reward or because he knew I would be mad at him if he ignored me. He turned to me because that is how a pack member behaves—when a secure structure is in place, they defer to pack members who hold a senior position for guidance. Unless you are a hunter, you are not likely to encounter such a high-stakes situation as we did with those coyotes. But you are likely to encounter many circumstances where it will benefit you to have this kind of connection with your dog.

THE DIFFERENCE BETWEEN BEHAVIOR AND TRAINING

There is a fundamental difference between working with behavior versus training a dog. Understanding this difference will go a long way to helping you make the changes you are looking for in your dog's actions.

A dog's behavior is a result of their genetic inheritance as a canine as well as their individual personality and experience. Behavior is natural and innate. When they feel safe and secure in their pack, and are able to fulfill their purpose, they exhibit well-adjusted behavior. When there is a structural insecurity, or they cannot do what they were meant to do, they will behave in ways that we likely perceive as troublesome. I studied wild canines for years, both in captivity and in the wild, to discover how dogs and wolves raise well-adjusted pack members in their natural environment. The responsibility falls in large part to mamma, who communicates with body language, species-specific pheromones, and other methods. While we cannot emulate many of the ways wild canines communicate, we can use their *expect, warn, correct* three-stage process to develop a harmonious relationship with them.

Here is how it works. The pack shares a set of expectations for how to be a contributing and productive pack member, but the youngsters do not know what those are yet. When they violate those expectations, mamma issues a warning. She may show her teeth, raise her hair, or vocalize in the form of a low growl in an attempt to give the puppy an opportunity to stop the undesirable behavior. In this moment, the offending pups have a choice. They can redirect their energy and "pass" the test or continue their behavior and "fail." If they fail, mamma will turn to physical correction as a means to discourage the behavior. She may nip them, swat at them, or physically pick them up and move them. (Adult canines behave the same way—warning each other through body language and vocalizations before resorting to physical correction. The difference here is that adults will take things to an escalated level in a way that a mamma will not do with her pups.)

This choice-based method of working with behavior is not about modifying or forcing them to act in a specific way. It is about conveying the norms of the community while simultaneously allowing room for each individual to be who they are. It is about establishing the boundaries of what is permitted and what is not—and in doing so, it creates a respect for the structure and increases the security of the pack, which increases the odds of survival. Once a pack member understands where the edges of acceptable behavior are, they are then free to behave as the unique being that they are within those parameters. They can be rambunctious, aggressive, playful, goofy, nurturing, quiet, or mellow—however it suits them. And they are encouraged to fulfill their purpose as a hunter, herder, or protector within the limits of what is acceptable.

Training, on the other hand, is quite different than working with behavior. It is about channeling, shaping, or funneling a dog's behavior so they can integrate comfortably into human society. It takes their natural abilities and steers them into ways of acting that work for us while simultaneously giving them a way to cope with this strange world that they find themselves in. While it is an important way to help dogs coexist safely with us, our modern day training methods do not usually serve to allow a dog to be authentically who they are. In that sense, training has no purpose in the dog's life—nothing in their evolution prepared them for a need to sit, stay, or roll over, thus training itself rarely satisfies their natural impulses.

Training routines are based on a *command, mark, release* method that is uniquely human because it is based exclusively on verbal communication and is about unnatural tasks. Training involves issuing a task or a command like "sit," "stay," or "come"; marking the moment when they obey by saying something like "good boy," "good girl," or "yes"; and releasing them from the task with a word like "okay," "out," or "release". In many cases, the release is followed by a food reward. Training is unnatural because canines would never communicate with each other like this in the wild. Mamma would never speak a command and would never approve or disapprove of them based on their obedience. More importantly, she would never reward them with food.

Although they are two very different approaches, behavior and training complement each other in many ways. Training is crucial to the development of behavior. It bridges the gap between canine behavior and human behavior by giving both parties a common goal to work toward. And behavior is critical to training because it develops the respect necessary to give you some level of authority. If you do not have any authority, then your dog will not listen to you when you want to train them. Or, they will listen to you when they want the food you are offering as a reward, but will ignore you if they are not hungry or if they decide something else in the situation supersedes your offer.

It is possible to have a really well-trained dog with behavioral issues. They may be willing to do anything for food, but they may also be extremely neurotic and unhappy, living a life quite divorced from their purpose. It is also possible to have a well-behaved dog who is terrible at following direct commands. Your job as a provider is to find the balance of behavior and training that allows your furry family member to lead a satisfying life while fitting into the particular circumstances of your pack. With a little effort, you can create a safe space to live and work together and break down some of the barriers to communication between our species.

BEHAVIOR   **TRAINING**

BEHAVIOR	TRAINING
Expect, Warn, Correct	Command, Mark, Release
✿	✿
Is Natural to Them	Is Unnatural and Based on Human Rules
✿	✿
Communicates Boundaries	Requests Completion of a Specific Task
✿	✿
Leaves Room for Individuality	Looks for Conformity
✿	✿
Canine-centric	Human Centric
✿	✿
Establishes Respect for Structure	Establishes Human Guidance
✿	✿
Purpose Unfolds Naturally	Helps Them Live Their Purpose

Understanding the difference between working with behavior and training a dog will help you create a harmonious pack.

THE CHOICE-BASED BEHAVIOR ROUTINE

In the remainder of this chapter, we will explore how we can emulate the canine's natural expect, warn, correct process to create a clear sense of structure and safety for your pack. We will explore how we can help them understand the world they live in without suppressing their natural way of being. Then, in the following chapter, we will turn our attention to training.

With those ideas in mind, here's the basic choice-based behavior routine. First, I will outline the process and provide a general explanation of the approach, followed by some routines for specific issues.

1. Test and Present the Scenario

2. Vocal Warning

3. Physical Correction or Guidance

4. Vocal Acceptance

5. Release

TEST AND PRESENT THE SCENARIO: Leash the dog and then hold the leash loosely. Bring the dog into a situation where they may not know what to do, but do not give them any instructions. Remain calm and have a clear expectation of how you wish them to behave in this situation. If it helps, think of yourself as a mamma wolf. At this point in the process, you must sit back and observe, giving them room to make their own decision. It can be hard to wait, but it is important to allow them the choice. You do not want to provoke them or force them to do something, but you do want them to be compelled to make a decision. Giving them the room to make a choice is how they learn, and it allows us to gather information about their natural desires and individual personality.

VOCAL WARNING: If they fail the test and do not behave as you expect them to, it is time for a pre-escalated vocalization. Mamma will use a number of vocal and non-vocal ways of communicating a warning, but we have only one primary means: our voice. I keep it simple and say, "Hey! or "Hep!" then give them a second to make their choice again. Patience is key at this stage, as you want to give them the chance to acknowledge your authority and follow through with meeting your expectation.

PHYSICAL CORRECTION: If they do not react to your vocal warning in the way you wish them to, then you need to respond with a physical intervention like mamma would. My primary means of correction is by "popping" the leash. This can take some practice, because you are going for a clear and firm correction, but you want to do it softly enough that you do not hurt the dog. Use the amount of force that is equal to tapping the dog clearly but gently on the shoulder. Think of the leash and the collar as an extension of your hand, and if you are not going to hurt the dog with your hand, then you are not going to hurt them with the leash, so pop gently but firmly enough to translate your intentions.

It is especially important at this stage to be in control of your emotions. Dogs can sense your emotional state, and if you yank the leash with anger or frustration, they will know. Using fear and inflicting pain has no place in a healthy relationship. But providing clear communication using an approach they are familiar with—physical touch—does.

Keep popping the leash until your dog stops what they are doing and looks at you. Sometimes they will respond immediately, but sometimes it may take a while, which means you will need to be patient and remain clear about what you are asking. There have been times when I have had to pop a leash for 30 minutes or more. It can be easy to get frustrated and lose your temper, so having practices to keep yourself calm is essential.

Some of my clients have described this approach as yogic, and to maintain this level of groundedness in yourself will likely require you to do some work on yourself. In Chapter 2, we learned about practices like mindfulness and meditation. Now is when those practices really pay off. If you maintain an even-keeled presence, they will learn that you are not going to cross a threshold with them. They do not need to fear you, but they recognize your insistence will outlast their stubbornness, which will make you the clear leader in the end.

VOCAL ACCEPTANCE: In the wild, canines do not give each other verbal praise. Instead, they show their appreciation through other means, such as grooming. When a mamma redirects a misbehaving pup and they acquiesce, she will often start licking them or cleaning their ears. Since that is not an option across our species, once your dog responds to the popping by looking at you, acknowledge their choice with a verbal behavioral marker. I typically say, "Good boy!" or "Good girl!" a few times, in a calm, measured tone.

You are not releasing the dog with this declaration; you are not giving them permission to get the food or chase the squirrel or whatever it is they wanted to do. Giving praise in this case acts as more like a confirmation of their behavior choice to look to you for guidance. By popping the leash, you escalated the situation, building up some tension as a subtle battle of wills ensued with the dog. Your verbal marker de-escalates the situation and lets the dog know that everything is good, that you are happy with their choice, that they are doing a good job, and that you want this behavior to continue. If they take their eyes off you and resume their agenda, take a step or two back from your desired target and begin the process again with a "Hey!" and then pop the leash if they do not respond to the vocal warning.

RELEASE: When you are confident the dog is deferring to your instruction, and you are ready to let them proceed, you will want to give them a clear signal. I think of this as the light switch effect. When you have an expectation (like do not touch that food), the light switches on. When you are ready to release them from that expectation, it is like switching the light off. Again, you will use a verbal instruction to help make this clear to them. I use "okay" because it is simple and easy and fits smoothly into my vocabulary, but you can choose any word you like. Some people use words like "free" or "out" or "all done." Whatever word you choose, the sentiment you are expressing is that you are the provider and you are now giving them permission to take whatever it was that they were being tested with, whether it is food or space on a couch, etc. You are delivering the message that you are in charge, and when they defer to you they will be taken care of.

IMPORTANT THINGS TO KNOW BEFORE YOU TRY THIS AT HOME

One size does not fit all. Over decades of working with tens of thousands of dogs, one of the most important lessons I have learned is that one size does not fit all. Every dog is unique, and they each behave how they do for very individual reasons. Even if two dogs seem to be behaving similarly, showing their teeth, for example, the causes of that behavior could be completely different. A dog might show their teeth out of aggression, fear, or pain, or in the course of play. So the first guideline is to pay close attention to the dog in front of you, observing and listening to them in an effort to hear what they are trying to say. Do not make any assumptions. Learn to become responsive to what is in front of you rather than blindly applying a routine.

Say calm, centered, and in charge. In working with behavior, you are intentionally escalating a situation. You are putting your dog in a situation where they will be forced to come to terms with who is in charge. Since you are intentionally provoking them, even a little, it is important that you commit to taking a peaceful, non-aggressive approach. Yes, you are establishing your role as a provider, but claiming power through fear or violence will not result in a well-adjusted dog. Your true power will come from remaining calm and asserting your authority with an even-keeled, consistent, and persistent approach.

Set your dog up for success. As you set up scenarios to work on behavior, you will also want to set your dog up for success. Do not go straight for their most difficult issue or start in a high-energy environment. And definitely do not push them. If they start to growl, show their teeth, or exhibit any other pre-escalated behaviors, do not continue to provoke them. Much like humans, they will not learn anything if they are triggered into a state of high arousal, so stop the process, de-escalate the situation, and then try again with an easier scenario or at a greater distance from the trigger. For example, if they act aggressively around other dogs or get possessive around their food bowl, start with something else that is a lower priority or try a walking routine instead.

Corrections should not be painful. Often when people start to work with my method, they worry about the use of physical correction. They think of emulating wild canines and visions of violent, bloody battles for dominance float through their minds, usually the memories of dramatic wildlife documentaries they saw when they were young. That is not the norm in wild canine behavior. Sure, it happens occasionally in the case of a major structural battle among fully developed adults, but far more often corrections are mild and to the point, and that is the approach we want to emulate. You are not looking to get into a structural battle with your dog. You are looking to communicate with them in a way that will make sense to them and that also leaves their natural attitude intact, even if that is a dominant, confident, alpha-type mentality. Well-placed physical corrections, using the same gentleness as mamma would, are communicative and supportive. To ensure you are using gentle pressure, hold the leash as loosely as you possibly can. If your dog is a flight risk, then try to work in an area that is contained so you can have a loose hold.

Use an eight- or ten-foot leash and a collar, not a harness. I prefer to use a collar over a body harness because the neck is the strongest part of a dog's body and communicating with a leash pop to the neck emulates how mamma targets her communication with her pups. I especially like the martingale collars, which have a large loop that goes around their neck and a smaller loop where you attach the leash. When you quickly and gently pop the leash, the collar compresses, delivering a gentle pressure to the dog's neck. These collars are difficult for dogs to wiggle out of, which is a benefit if you are working with dogs who have smaller heads, like Greyhounds and Dachshunds, or if you have a fearful dog that likes to back out of collars and harnesses. I am not a fan of prong collars, as they are too likely to cause the dog pain. While fear is a motivator, it is not the motivator you want to use to develop a trusting relationship with your dog.

What if your dog will not even tolerate being on the leash? I once worked with a dog who, as the leash was clicked on, would begin to scream and writhe as if someone was torturing her. She was not being aggressive—she did not try to bite me or lunge at me—it was clearly a tantrum. My approach was to try passive restraint by holding the leash out at arm's length with gentle pressure upward to keep the leash taught and not reacting. I kept myself calm and just let her work it out herself on the other end of the leash, which I held a few feet away from my body. And when she finished, I asked her to do what I wanted her to do anyway. If she went into a tantrum again, I let her do her thing and I remained a mountain—impassive and accepting and clear in my expectations.

This dog knew exactly what I wanted her to do, but her tantrum showed me she thought she was dominant. Eventually, she realized she was not going to win this battle. Because I did not react by meeting her energy in a negative way, she began to trust me. Once she gave in, I gave her everything she wanted, and she never challenged me or her human pack again. Today she is 100% off-leash, is a brilliant frisbee player, and is a superb deer shed (antler) dog. Not all dogs who have trouble being on leash will respond this way. Again, the dog in front of you is unique. If there is any sign of aggression toward you, do not force them. Seek the assistance of a professional.

DON'T PUSH THEM OVER THE THRESHOLD

An important aspect of working with behavior is learning how to provoke a choice without triggering them into aggressive or violent behavior. If you ever hire a trainer to assist you, and the first thing they do is provoke your dog to the point of escalation, consider looking for another trainer. If someone tells me their dog has food aggression, I may begin by throwing some food on the floor to see what they do. If they show even the slightest disregard, maybe just giving me a dirty look, I turn and walk away and let them have the food. I learned what I needed to learn—the dog does not respect my authority. Getting into a battle with this dog, provoking them to their most aggressive state, will not help. Instead, I will look for scenarios where this dog can pass or fail, but where things will not escalate into a barking or biting frenzy.

In the last chapter, I mentioned the scale I use to assess how much aggression a dog is exhibiting. The scale is from 1 to 100, and anything below 50 is considered pre-escalated behavior, which includes targeting posture, neutral or playful vocalizations, and body language. At some point, the dog's behavior escalates past the 50 mark, entering the territory of escalated behaviors. That is when you want to back off. Escalated behaviors may include challenging stares, protective stances, growling, barking, getting physically aggressive, or showing fear. Even attitudes like aloofness or disinterest can actually be a passive-aggressive sign of dominance. Each dog has a unique set of escalated behaviors, and your job is to learn the nuances of the dog you are working with.

To make a behavior change, you must work below the 50 threshold, or you will get nowhere. When a dog flips from pre-escalated to escalated behaviors, they can rocket to 100 in a split second, so you do not want to push them beyond 50. The escalated state is like a child throwing a tantrum—no learning happens, and those around them could get hurt if they interfere. Let the dog have its tantrum on its own, and when they are settled and calm again, you can negotiate and communicate.

Provoking a behavior without going too far can take some finesse, so be patient. Because each dog is an individual, what it takes to push them over the threshold will be different, so there are not a clear set of instructions to offer beyond reiterating the point that one size does not fit all. You will have to increase your powers of observation and attention and get to know your dog well. Over time, you will start to learn the particular signals that indicate you are pushing your dog too hard.

For example, if you wanted to work with your dog on letting them know they are not allowed on the bed, you do not want to put a leash on them while they are already asleep on your duvet. They have already claimed the space and are settled in, and if they give you the side-eye when you walk in the room, or they start to growl if you get close, they have already passed the 50 mark and are showing escalated behavior.

To work on this behavior, you will want to stage the scenario another time and in another place. If they do not feel possessive about the couch, and you are okay with them jumping up on it, start there. What you are aiming for is to get them to look to you for clarity of where it is okay and not okay for them to go. That can be practiced in many settings that are not as triggering as the bed, and the lessons learned elsewhere will eventually translate to this setting. Remember, every dog is different, so you will need to find the sweet spot for you and yours.

If you are working with a dog that is particularly aggressive, you might want to consider using a supplement like CBD, treats containing tryptophan, or other herbal supplements to calm them down a little. While I am not a big fan of pharmaceutical drugs, I find supplements can help to take the edge off and give you just enough wiggle room to start working with a dog. As always, check with your veterinarian before giving any supplement to your dog.

It is important to note that a dog can also go from zero to 100 in a heartbeat, although this typically happens with people they do not see as members of their pack. If your dog is triggered easily and you cannot find a way to keep them under 50 to work the routines, then there is a question of acceptance and I strongly suggest finding an animal behavior specialist to assist you.

A SIMPLE WALKING ROUTINE

To get comfortable with the choice-based behavior method, it can help to work with a routine that is straightforward and nonthreatening to most dogs. This walking routine will give you an opportunity to work on your leash technique and get familiar with how your dog responds in a low-energy-environment. (Note that if your dog is particularly aggressive when on a leash in any circumstance, this may not be the place to begin. Remember, every dog is different, and you will need to find your way with your pup.)

The goal of this routine is to get your dog to keep you in their awareness at all times and to follow your lead. Since the pack is the source of all safety, food, and love, you want them to identify you as the provider of the pack so they will be willing to go wherever you decide to go. Your expectation as the pack's provider is they will follow your lead—I call this the "roaming drive." If you picture a wolf pack, when the leaders get up and start to walk, the others automatically follow. There is no negotiation, no demands or cajoling from the provider—there is an intrinsic motivation to stay together, and that is what we are tapping into here.

1. Hold the leash loosely and begin to walk. The dog can walk on the right or the left, ahead of or behind you. (It can sometimes be more difficult to sense if a dog is still tuned into you if they are in front of you and looking at the ground. If it is too hard to evaluate that at the beginning, try to work with the dog closer to you.)

2. Take a few steps and then change direction, making a sharp turn. If the dog comes with you, great. If there is resistance, say, "Hey!" just once. Keep the leash loose, as if it is not even there.

3. If they still will not follow you, begin to pop the leash until they walk toward you.

4. Affirm their decision by saying "Good dog!"

As you continue to walk, pay attention to the moments when they want to go in their own direction. Maybe they want to go mark a tree or sniff a fire hydrant or greet another person. Change direction, walking away from their goal, and follow through with a "Hey!" and a pop. Once they follow you, say, "Good dog!" and immediately reverse direction and take them to the object they wanted. The message you are giving to them is that going to the tree or the hydrant or the person is fine, but it has to happen on your terms, and they have to go there with you, together, not dragging you behind them.

If your dog spends all their time at the very end of the leash pulling to go where they want to go, just turn your body and walk in a different direction. They know they are pulling, but you can let them know that you still have the expectation that they are going to follow you. Just repeat the process: give them a moment to make the choice; say "Hey!", pop the leash, and offer praise when they follow.

You will notice that this routine does not involve any shouting, pleading, nagging, yelling, tugging, dragging, or forcefulness. A dog's keen hearing means they will hear a simple "Hey!" without you raising your voice, and the gentle pop of the leash is the indication you want them to do something they are not doing yet. This method is a quiet approach that requires you to remain calm and patient.

A ROUTINE FOR THE TERRITORIAL/POSSESSIVE DOG

One of the most common complaints I get from people is that their dog is resource guarding. But when I meet families, I often find that the problem is actually a lack of clarity around the pack/family hierarchy. When a dog protects food, water, or pack from *outside influences,* that is considered resource guarding. These things are critical to survival, and they will defend them to the death in the wild, if necessary. When a dog guards their food or an area, a bone, a stick, a blanket, or a toy from someone *within the pack or family,* that is not resource guarding—it is an issue of possession. If a dog has been fed twice a day, every day, for 10 years, then there is no need for them to sit protectively over their empty food bowl. If they do, they are simply being possessive or territorial and saying, "This is mine...do not touch it!" or "leave this area now." They are asserting their authority over you via controlling this item or the area.

Why is this distinction important? While resource guarding and possessiveness are both behavior responses, the way to work with them is different. With resource guarding, you will want to work with the dog's fear (lack of confidence); with possessiveness, you will want to work with the dog's dominance (confidence). However, both behaviors will require that you work with a routine based on structure and communication. If your dog truly has an issue with resource guarding, working directly with food may be quite risky. Instead, I would start with some back-end work on pack trust, which should remedy the situation.

If your dog is territorial, it can help to do some work ahead of the behavior routine. In one case, an owner called me because their dog was "resource guarding" his toys. When I evaluated the dog, he exhibited mild aggression around his toys—he would growl and show his teeth, but he would not bite if you tried to take the toy. It was obvious to me this was an issue of possession (structure). In order to work on getting the dog to realize who was in charge, I had to first find a way to get the dog to not be so provoked around toys.

My strategy was to try a form of immersion therapy and flood the dog with more toys than he knew what to do with. I had the family give the dog a new toy every day for two weeks. At some point, there were so many toys around that the dog lost interest. It was no longer an issue if you took one of his toys because there was another one nearby. This did not address the bigger behavioral issue, but it lowered the stakes for working on the problem. Now the dog was much less on edge and I could begin to stage behavior routines, taking a toy and saying, "Hey, this is mine," using the leash, warning with "Hey!" and correcting with "pops." I have done similar things with dogs who are resource guarding around food—giving them more food with a steady scheduled feeding routine and, over time, they develop a positive expectation and begin to value it less. When the stakes get lowered, I start to work on the relationship through developing communication and establishing my provider position.

If you wish to let your dog know that you are in charge of the food, start with throwing down a small, bite-sized piece of something that they feel has lesser value (like a piece of kibble instead of bacon). If you see any adverse reactions—like growling, barking, lunging, biting at the leash—just let them have it. At this point, you may want to consult with an animal behaviorist to troubleshoot how to work with your dog. I guarantee you there is a way in, but you may need help to see it.

If there are no signs of aggressive behavior present, then try this routine:

1. Put the leash on your dog and then toss a small piece of food onto the floor beyond the distance of the length of the leash. Give them a chance to pass or fail. Do not say anything at this point. Do not use sit, stay, leave it, or any other commands. Just give them a simple choice to pass or fail.

2. If the dog moves to take the food, say, "Hey!"

3. If they do not stop and look at you, pop the leash repeatedly until they do. If they have gone to the full length of the leash, loosen it enough to get a pop. Remember, the leash and the collar are an extension of your hand, so think of yourself as tapping them with gentle, subduing pressure. Stick with it as long as you need to. You are escalating the situation here, so keep an eye on your dog's cues to make sure you do not push them over the threshold.

4. When they make eye contact, it is time to de-escalate by using a calm behavioral marker like "Good dog!" a few times. Be

sure to reflect your pleasure in the tone of your voice but remain calm and low energy—you want to reinforce their behavior and make them feel good about their decision to look at you.

5. When you are ready, release them with an "Okay!" or "Free!" and allow them to have the food. You can pet them and bring the energy levels up a bit. If done correctly, the release should be the hardest part. They may need a little encouragement to take the food. Just flick the food toward them and say, "Okay!" Do not pick up the food and give it to them—you are not looking to reward them. You are providing them with something out of our love for them.

The goal of this routine is to let the dog know whose territory this is and whose food this is. You are giving them the message that you are in charge and that you will provide. With training commands like "leave it," you need to be present and hyper-aware of every stick and every piece of popcorn your dog comes across. By establishing a structure where your dog looks to you or waits for your permission, there is much more balance in the pack. And you can take advantage of any moment when they look to you or not touch food to give them the ultimate reward: love and affection.

CUSTOMIZING YOUR APPROACH

The choice-based behavior routine is just one way to work with behavior. I know I have said it a lot in this chapter, but each dog is unique, and when you are working with behavior it is not one-size-fits-all. There are no routines suited to every dog. There is no one explanation for each behavior. Not everyone is comfortable with this level of nuance, but I believe it is more honest and reflects and respects the complexity of the beings we are living with.

Like human psychology, there are general principles of dog psychology that can be applied to canines. But also, like humans, where not every person with depression is the same, not all dogs will present the same way. You have to take the time to learn about each individual, their pack dynamics, and their current and past environment. Do not assume you can just work the steps and get the results you are looking for. There is an infinite number of variables that could make your situation unique or even contraindicated to the routines I have described above. Your situation may require some creative thinking, and that is where it pays to work with a professional. Going into that working relationship with an understanding that every dog and situation is a unique puzzle to solve will set you all up for success.

You can never modify the nature of a dog. You can only understand it,
appreciate it, encourage it, and manage it. By doing so, you create a safe,
happy, healthy, and loving life for another being to live out their full potential.
—David J. Kurlander

6

Training: An Unnatural Approach

You may find it strange that we have gotten all the way to Chapter 6 before we even begin to address what most people think of as the fundamentals of dog training: teaching them to sit, stay, and come. But to get to the point where you can successfully train a dog requires that you lay the groundwork of the previous chapters first. You must begin with establishing parameters for good behavior by using structure and communication to convey to your dog that they are safe, loved, and provided for within the pack. Trying to train a dog without this foundation is futile. If a dog is aggressive or fearful, if they are uncertain or lack confidence, if they do not know who is in charge or where their next meal is coming from, they will not be predisposed to learning. Just like kids in school, dogs will thrive and learn easily in a safe, stable, and predictable environment.

Once you have established a secure structure and made your expectations about behavior clear, you can begin to train your dog to do any number of things—from basic commands to more complex tasks. You may want to train your dog with a few simple instructions or teach them to do something more sophisticated like hunting; protection sports like Schutzhund, French Ring, or Belgian Ring; service work like bomb-sniffing, drug-sniffing, or search and rescue; or pulling a sled. This kind of training is only possible if there is a solid structure in place, which is why I always stress to people to work on behavior first.

Before I talk about training, I want to clarify that I am an animal behavior specialist. Although I train domestic canines for upland and waterfowl hunting, there is a fundamental difference between what I do with a family and what most "dog trainers" do. I am concerned with helping dogs live out the meaning and purpose of their life. I want them to be able to freely express their individual personality safely and comfortably. I work with individuals and other professionals in the animal field to help families understand how they can best offer their furry family member this opportunity. My work incorporates a scientific and spiritual approach that honors a dog's evolutionary heritage and the mystery of what it is like to experience life through their eyes.

You may think it is splitting hairs to make this distinction between trainers and behaviorists, but there can be significant differences in how we approach working with dogs. In this chapter, I will explain how I use the principles of training to support my behavioral approach. I will also offer my perspective on some of the popular training methods and beneficial devices out there. While I think some approaches are more effective than others, any positive approach to training will produce some results. Why? Because effort matters. As we discussed in Chapter 4, if you pay attention to the needs of another being, they tend to respond positively. Any effort you make will not go unrewarded, but with the right technique, training can be far more than party tricks—it can support your dog in satisfying their natural purpose.

WHY DO WE TRAIN DOGS?

Even though I do not prefer to work in the capacity of a professional dog trainer outside of my hunting focus, I believe training is important because it helps bridge the gap between canine behavior and human behavior by giving dogs and humans a common goal. If I am going to take my dog hunting, they need to learn how we hunt as humans. I will not be hunting in the same way my dog's wild pack mates will, so I will need a way to communicate to them how we can successfully hunt together. This is where training comes in. As you work toward achieving something specific together, spending hours doing positive and encouraging work through consistent routines, you also develop trust and deepen your bond with each other.

Additionally, training helps dogs navigate this strange human world they live in. While incredibly adaptable, tens of thousands of years of evolution did not prepare dogs for living indoors, dodging cars, or having random strangers walk into the safety of their den. Training is a form of communication that can close the gap between our two worlds and give them the means of understanding what is expected of them to be successful in the human world.

In my philosophy, training is a tool. Much like a hammer, you can use training to create something special—something that goes above and beyond the simple tool itself. For example, you can use a hammer to build a house. But you can also use it to knock one down. The same tool, used with different intentions, can create radically different outcomes. Training can help you build a harmonious pack, or it can be simply transactional—you do what I ask, and I give you a reward. Even worse, it can be used to suppress or attempt to change the true nature of a dog—efforts that will rarely satisfy anyone in the pack and run completely counter to my philosophy.

INTENTION IS THE KEY

Once a dog has an understanding of basic commands like "sit,"
"stay," "come," and "lay down," you can develop training
routines to fulfill their inherent genetic impulses and enhance or
influence their behavior. The stacked stress routine covered later
in this chapter is a great example of using training to affect
behavior. However, simply learning basic commands is not going
to satisfy your dog in the long run. Mastering "sit," "stay," or
"come" will not in any way help them to live out their purpose to
hunt, herd, or protect. And it will not resolve any behavioral
issues. If used properly, training methods can help reinforce
structure by giving you an opportunity to establish or assert your
authority as a pack provider. But you must use these training
methods with that intention in mind, otherwise, you are just
asking a dog to do party tricks.

The ultimate goal of training is to get you to the point where the
dog can be safely off-leash so they can freely perform the

activities they are born to do. I often have people say to me that for years their dog was so well trained and then they just stopped listening. Dogs need constant, deep mental stimulation, and after a while, for many dogs, performing on command for a treat will rapidly lose its value. It would be as if you were to simply go to work at a job that you have little to no interest in. You would have zero internal satisfaction and would probably feel stuck and miserable. The moment something more interesting is offered, you would leave that job without hesitation. Neither you nor your dog is simply out for the reward (money for you, treats for them)—what will make you both feel a sense of accomplishment and meaning is to fulfill your innermost desires and live your purpose. That is the truest reward.

Training is a means to an end. Do you know what the end goal is for the dog you are working with? Do you know what it is that makes them happy to be alive? I had a Labrador who was obsessed with hunting. If a duck went down in the water, he would jump in and swim right to it, like a shark on prey. But if I threw a ball in the water, he would stand at the edge and whine. He was a hunter, not a swimmer. The ball was clearly not a bird and was in no way going to satisfy his natural instincts. Neither would be jumping in the lake for a recreational swim, which I never saw him do.

Alternatively, my current Labrador, Ásgeirr, will jump in the water for anything. If I throw a rock in, he will dive underwater to find it. No matter what the object, retrieving is his thing, and being in the water brings him immense joy. Given the difference in personalities and preferences of these two individuals, I approached their training routines with the mindful intention of using their strengths to develop confidence and create habits that set them up for success. Many approaches to training focus on weaknesses, but I find when I focus on strengths, the "weaknesses" fade away with little to no effort. As with everything related to your dog, think of things through their eyes and get creative with how you use training to give them a more satisfying life. But to get there, let us start with the basics.

COMMAND, MARK, AND RELEASE

In the previous chapter, we described the differences between behavior and training. Working with behavior consists of getting to know a dog on a deeper level, as an individual with a depth of emotions and soul, not just as your "pet." Behavior is about understanding a dog's natural ways of relating and creating routines based on how they communicate with each other in the wild: expect, warn, and correct.

With training, the process begins with a different assumption— that we are asking them to do something unnatural. Anything you want a dog to do that they would not be expected to do in their wild pack would fall under the category of training. If you cannot imagine mama wolf requiring it of her pups, then you are firmly in the territory of training, not behavior. For example, I have never seen a wolf ask another wolf to "sit," "stay," "lay down," or "fetch the ball."

Because we are working with something that they do not have any context for evolutionarily speaking, we follow a different process. Instead of expect, warn, and correct, we use verbal cues that follow a human-contrived scenario: command, mark, and release. The truly amazing thing is that our dogs catch on so quickly and are eager to work with us to do these things that nature did not prepare them for. To understand how incredible this is, imagine the reverse scenario. Could you live with a pack of canines and understand them even a fraction of the amount that they have come to understand us? I could not. For more than 25 years, I have been diligently studying animal behavior and working hand-in-hand with a variety of species of animal beings, and I can confirm none are more willing to be a part of our lives than dogs are. And I feel as if I have just dipped my toe into the ocean of mystery and potential that this special relationship holds.

My approach to training utilizes the same light switch effect that I use in working with behavior. It is a communication technique that uses energy levels to reinforce what is being asked of the dog in any given moment. Remember, dogs communicate using emotion and energy. If you want to have the upper hand as a pack provider, you have to learn to do the same. When you give a command, it is like turning on the light switch. When you release them, it is like turning it off. If you master this, your dog will learn to match your energy and follow your lead all the time, not just when you are doing a training routine.

Here is the basic process:

Command. With the dog on a leash, speak your command to them. It does not matter what language you use, and you can eventually use different words or a series of words to identify the same command. But start with one simple word for the sake of consistency and ease of learning, and use a tone of voice that is confident, neutral, and commands respect. When you state your command and turn the light switch on, you ask them to be alert and focused on you for the next instruction, and you must reflect that level of alertness in yourself. Your tone should provoke anticipation. You want them to focus on you as if they are saying, "What's next? What exciting thing are we going to do now? How can I be part of it?"

If you have a strong connection with the dog, they will know you are asking them to do something. They will feel a gradual increase in stress as they try to figure out what it is you want. Be sure to be clear about your intentions and consistently follow through each time. You may have to repeat the process a few times, so stay patient until you achieve the results you are looking for. Each dog has their own learning curve, and the more patience you have, the easier it will become for them to learn.

When you give them a command for the first time, be clear in your intention and see what happens. Give them a chance to intuit what you are asking and to follow your request. If they do not understand what you are asking, you may need to ask again and offer some gentle direction or guiding encouragement to show them what you want. For example, if you are asking them to sit, place your hand on their back end and with gentle pressure (no more than the weight of your hand itself), and keep asking them to sit until they do. Be more stubborn than they are, but do not use force. If you have already put in the work to establish a solid understanding of structure, their rear will usually drop to the floor quite effortlessly. If you want them to lay down, you might need to direct them with the leash. Whatever you are asking them to do, do not push or force them. If there is resistance, then you may have a dominance issue or a dog with a fearful aversion of your hands, which is a behavioral problem, and you may want to return to working with a routine to establish structure.

Mark. As soon as they do what you have asked, immediately mark their success with verbal reinforcement. I prefer "Good boy" or "Good girl", but you can use any phrase. This communicates to them that they accomplished what you asked them to do. Your tone of voice should be positive, but soft, calm, and even-keeled. You are de-escalating the situation and taking

271

off some of the pressure that you put on them with your initial request, but you are not relieving it completely—the light switch is still on. You simply want to reassure them that they got it right and you appreciate that, but you still have them in a holding pattern, waiting for another command or to be released.

Note that your mark does not release them. I often see dogs stand up when they hear "Good dog", mostly because the person's energy changes, escalating to the point where the dog thinks the light switch has been turned off and they are free to go about their business. But marking is simply an indication that what they are doing is correct and that you want them to continue doing it. So, keep your energy even and just give them a "Good" or some other word that connects emotionally and is equivalent to how you might answer them if they had literally asked the question, "Is this what you want me to do?" You are just confirming that indeed they got it right. Avoid petting them at this stage, as affection is a form of reward that might prematurely release them.

I have had some clients ask if they should avoid saying "Good dog!" when working routines because they want to be able to say, "What a good dog!" throughout the day, unassociated with particular requests. A dog's emotional life is far more complex than most people think. They can tell the difference between circumstances, and, in fact, developing a positive association with the phrase "Good boy" or "Good girl" by using it at times outside training will help them recognize your positive feelings when you use it as a marker.

Release. To release them, choose an easy word to indicate they have successfully fulfilled your request and they are now free to move about of their own will. I like to use the word "Okay!" as it is easy, familiar, and makes sense, but you can pick something that rolls off your tongue or that you like to use to generate enthusiasm. Releasing them turns the light switch off, so whatever word you choose, bring your energy level up and give them lots of affection and acknowledgment.

WHERE IS THE TREAT?

You may be thinking that this is the moment when a treat will finally appear in this process, but I do not encourage you to use food as a reward. Instead, the reward is attention, affection, and play. Play is an important part of a canine's life. It is one way a pack develops a healthy dynamic, as well as the necessary skills for survival. Through play, they learn a tremendous amount about rules, structure, hunting, protection, and discipline.

In the wild, the most important rule around play is the pack provider decides when and how play happens. Wolves communicate the terms through both overt and subtle body language. For example, an adult wolf may lay down and display their teeth, indicating that play is acceptable at that moment, but that boundaries must be respected. The younger pack member must maintain a level of awareness of the provider's cues during play. A provider needs to remain vigilant and pay attention to the surroundings. If they spot a deer at that moment and a younger member of the pack decides that is the moment to tussle with the provider, the pack could lose its only meal for the week. Young pups quickly learn not to solicit from the pack's providers uninvited.

Similarly, in our human-canine pack, I decide when we play. During the day, I will approach my dogs many times and have a quick session of play and affection, but I never allow them to solicit attention like that from me. This gives them the message that I am not to be interrupted at any time and lets me set the terms for our interactions. Play then becomes both a reward and an incentive. When I give my dogs a command, they quickly execute the instruction because they know once the release is given, and the light switch is turned off what will follow is some fun, connection, and bonding.

In addition to play, I will often use an exchange of items as a reward or incentive. Let us use retrieving as an example. If I want to ask a dog to find something like a disease, an illegal substance, or a person, they will not understand on a cognitive level why I am asking them to do that. I cannot appeal to their sense of reason in these circumstances like I can when they are hunting, where they are aware of the importance of the task at hand. Nor can I explain to them using words why it is important. But by making it fun, by bringing the energy of play to the exchange, I can create a scenario that satisfies their natural instincts while also serving us in some way.

When I start working with a dog to teach them to retrieve something, I will have an object of high value in hand that I know they will enjoy, like a ball, a rope toy, a frisbee, or a canvas retrieving bumper. I call these bridge objects. I want the dog to think that the objects are no fun without my participation, so I reserve these objects for specific events and never allow the dog to have them without my interaction. It is not so much the object that is important, it is the fact that they are a means of engaging in fun and play with me. When the dog brings back this unnatural object I am asking them to retrieve, they are motivated to deliver that item to me because they know I have another item of great interest that will get me to engage with them further. The interaction then becomes a two-way street: it is satisfying to me because they have done what I asked, and it is meaningful for them because they get to engage in continuous play with me. I will either throw the ball or play tug-of-war with them for a minute as a form of reward.

You may have experienced something different with your dog and toys. Some dogs will not bring the ball back at all or will stop 10 feet away and hope you will chase them. This may be because your dog was never taught how to play, and they are creating their own rules of the game. It could also be that the dog is being possessive. Either way, draw some guidelines and let them know you are the one to determine the rules. You can use a bridge item, like a ball, and when they come near, show them the second ball. When they realize it is the one you are going to play with, most of the time they will drop the one they have so they can continue to play with you.

If they want to play a game of chase, you can turn the tables on them by running away as they start to make their way back to you. Flip the game around so it is on your terms and make them chase you. Then try the exchange of items again, telling them to drop it or to sit. Having a long leash on the dog can also help to prevent the dog from darting off. Stepping on the leash will restrain the dog from running away as you continue encouraging the play routine. Be careful if you try to grab the leash as your dog begins to run away. Your instinct to stop them may result in a fairly significant rope burn on your hands if you have a large dog who is already barreling off in the other direction.

In this example, you can see how closely connected behavior and training are with each other. In fact, the line can feel very blurry sometimes. As I mentioned, I am not a dog trainer in the traditional sense, although I will use command, mark, release techniques when needed. I use the concepts from training to work with behavior. It can take some time to learn to discern between the two, but I encourage you to stick with it, as you will find it is a powerful approach to satisfying a dog's needs while getting them to do what you want them to do. One of my favorite routines for using training to modify or shape behavior is the stacked stress routine. But before we take a look at that, let us address why I do not find it useful to use food in training.

WHY I DO NOT SUGGEST TRAINING WITH FOOD

The most popular form of dog training is to use food as a temporary reward or positive reinforcement. I refer to this as the" vending machine" method: by performing a task, the dog gets a treat. It is like putting a dollar bill into a machine and out comes your candy bar. While it may work on a superficial level to train your dog to sit, stay, or come, there are several reasons why I do not use this approach.

First, I have never seen a wolf give another wolf a treat for acting a certain way. They do use food as a reward, but not in the way we think. When the providers make a kill, the more dominant dogs first communicate to the rest of the pack that this is their kill by growling and showing their teeth. After they have eaten their fill, which will ensure they can go hunt for the pack again, they allow the rest of the pack to eat. They do not just hoard the carcass for when they are hungry the next day—they reward the rest of the pack by providing food. This is an oversimplification, as pack dynamics are quite complex, but it is accurate enough for my point here.

I model my approach as much as I can on the ancient instincts and behaviors of wild canines, so if I want to use food as a reward, then showing my dog love and feeding them is how I would do it in a way that most resembles what they are used to evolutionarily. In my case, I give them their regularly scheduled meals as well as random special treats throughout the day without requiring them to do anything for it. We can observe this behavior in our own human families, as well—we feel compelled to share yummy treats with those we love more than with strangers.

Another reason I do not encourage people to use treat training is that it does not have a consistent effect on dogs. In general, I would say about 20% of dogs respond well to treat training. These dogs have just the right personality to make it work. They want to please, they are not obsessed with food, and they have little to no presence of a natural alpha mentality. They have no underlying behavior problems, so the training does not bring anything negative to light.

About 60% of dogs will respond to treat training, but not in the way you would hope. They will perform the task in particular environments, but the moment an outside force with higher priority comes into play, they will forget the treat and redirect their focus to what they think is more important. These dogs typically have dominant personalities and display strong leadership characteristics, but they do not have alpha mentalities. They are smart and seem to listen well most of the time, but then, often in a moment where it is important for their safety, they will ignore you and run off after an animal, chase a car, or jump on a guest.

I often get calls from confused clients who wonder why the dog is so good at following commands on the one hand and so badly behaved on the other. It is because this vending machine approach to food does not give them any cues about pack structure, nor does it communicate what is expected of them. Training your dog to simply "shake" or "roll over" is completely unrelated to the structure of the pack and their role in it. This is what I mean when I say training by itself is not going to give you the bond you need to have a truly harmonious pack.

Eighty percent of dogs are covered in the first two categories. The remaining 20% can be a real challenge because they will respond quite negatively to treat training. This includes aggressive dogs with strong alpha mentalities as well as fearful dogs. Dominance is not a bad thing in a dog. Dominant dogs have a lot of confidence and a great desire to partake in maintaining the security and survival of the pack. It is a characteristic you want in a hunting or protection dog, but this type of personality must be approached cautiously and nurtured properly.

When you reward a dominant dog with food for doing a simple action, you boost their ego, or their sense of self-importance, and they can get aggressive, biting your hand or demanding a treat at times when you are not even training. If you try to wean a dog off treats and they ignore your commands and nose your pockets for kibbles, they are exhibiting a lack of respect. If they steal your sock from the laundry and you give them a treat to get it back— or if you are eating dinner and the dog starts to perform unrequested tricks so they can get a bite of your hamburger—you are not the one in charge in this dynamic. In these cases, the dog is acting as an extortionist.

Please note that aggression does not necessarily translate into violence. A dog can be dominant and aggressive and never harm the ones they love. They may just utilize their presence with extreme mental stubbornness or with obnoxious physical force. If you are experiencing anything more than a forceful pup, you may want to take a step back and reevaluate your situation for the safety of yourself and everyone one else around you and seek assistance from an animal behavior specialist.

Fearful dogs can also respond negatively to treat training by getting aggressive because they perceive treat training as you trying to "pay them off." You are supposed to be the leader, someone they would follow without question, but instead, you are trying to pay them off to do a job. This is unsettling to them. People often use food as a method to lure fearful dogs into doing something that may put them in a vulnerable situation, like getting into their crate. This can cause serious mistrust and psychological trauma as they realize they have been tricked into doing something or being somewhere that makes them uncomfortable. Additionally, when a dog begins to hyper-focus on something, like the treat, their senses tune out other things around them such as perceived potential threats and the slightest disturbance to that focus could cause them to react in an aggressive panic.

When I say I am not a fan of treat training for most dogs, people often respond that it worked for their dog, and I say, "Great! I am glad!" But I am not so convinced that it works because of the training method itself. I attribute a great part of that success to effort. A good number of dogs will respond well to any positive training by making changes in their behavior simply because you are showing an effort to be part of their life. We all, human and animal alike, want to reciprocate when someone shows interest in us. I will sometimes tell clients that they can begin to get results by just paying attention to their pup. Take them for a walk or play with them every day. Any effort, no matter how small, will bring about change.

A few final observations about treat training. One of the first things many food-oriented training programs have you do is hold a piece of food and bring your hand up to between your eyes, saying something like, "Look at me." The idea is to get the dog to give you their attention and focus. I am sorry to say that even if they look you in the eyes, the dog's attention is on that food, not you. And even when you no longer use food (the idea with most food training is that you wean the dog off the food eventually and they will just obey at that point), people are often stuck having to bring their hand to their face to try to gain their dog's attention, and the dog is still not looking at them, they are looking for food.

This trick, along with the command "Leave it!", is unnecessary in my approach. As the pack provider, I am the center of the world for my dogs. They always have one eye on me, or one ear cocked my way—they always have me in their awareness—and they take their cues from me on what to do next. I do not need to force them to look at me because they already are, or they do so willingly when I ask them to. I do not need to tell them to "Leave it!" because they would not touch something without me giving them permission to touch it in the first place. And if they happen to approach something I do not want them to interact with, a simple, "Hey," which is a behavioral warning, will show my disapproval, and rarely do they ever approach that thing again.

THE "DO IT OR I'LL HURT YOU" METHOD

There is one more approach to training that I feel compelled to say something about, and those are the methods that fall under the heading of "do it or I will hurt you." This training approach is an outgrowth of the human parenting approach used on many of us over 40 years old: do what I say or I will smack you upside the head! These methods have no place in a healthy relationship, human or canine. There are, of course, healthy species-specific disciplinary actions, but the use of physical force to bend the will of others is not only counterproductive but fundamentally abusive.

Aggressive training methods often seem effective because they get results, but how you get results is far more important than just simply getting the result. Using physical pain or the threat of physical pain to make someone do something out of fear is not how you build respect. Sometimes a training method will downplay the pain it causes, saying it might give the dog some "discomfort," but this is deceiving. Some dogs may tolerate these methods and will not show their true emotions because they are stoic by nature, but let us not pretend what they are feeling is anything less than what it is. Pain is pain.

With these methods, the dog may obey, but not because they have a choice to do so and certainly not because they respect you as a leader. They will forge an unhealthy bond with you similar to what is described in humans as Stockholm Syndrome, where someone does what they are asked to do, no matter how horrific, because they know their survival depends on it. They comply with the instruction because they are broken and little is left of who they truly are. This is an abhorrent situation for humans and dogs.

Pack leaders should be the ultimate provider of safety. In the wild, pack leaders do not hurt other pack members. Yes, there are occasionally battles between two psychologically mature adults over structural disagreements—and on rare occasions these battles may even be deadly—but no healthy pack leader uses violence to get other pack members to behave, especially not their young. Since our domesticated dogs never exit the juvenile state of existence psychologically, the model I prefer to emulate is how mamma wolf would treat her pups. We must respond appropriately, correcting with patience and in a way that directs but does not suppress their natural personalities.

THE STACKED STRESS ROUTINE

Once your dog has a basic command of sit, stay, and come, you can use something that I call the stacked stress routine to reinforce that you are the pack leader and solidify your leadership. In this routine, you add one stressor on top of another as a way of conditioning the dog to listen to you no matter what. It builds awareness and focus and is a routine I often use to get to know a dog. It reveals their tolerance for unpredictability and how ready they are to defer to your authority. It is also a great example of how to use training commands to influence something like structure and communication. It uses the principle of operant conditioning, which employs either reward or punishment (in my case, reward) to reinforce behavior by getting the dog to associate the reward with their behavior.

To start this routine, begin by issuing the command to sit. The command itself turns the light switch on and generates a small amount of stress—let us say it takes the dog from a zero to a two on the scale of stress. When the dog sits, mark their compliance with a "good dog" to acknowledge their correct response. This de-escalates the command and reduces the stress slightly, but since you have not released them completely, there is still some uncertainty on their part. Let us say at this point they have dropped down to a one on the stress scale. Now give the dog another command, like "come." This adds another two to our scale, so we are now at a three. When the dog comes, acknowledge it with a marker, which in turn brings it down to two on the scale, and then issue another command.

As you can see, the longer you give commands without releasing or rewarding the dog, the higher you climb on the ladder of stress. If you go two steps up the ladder for every one step down, you increase the stress level, putting more pressure on the dog to keep up with you. It is as if the light switch is a dimmer and you are going up some and down a little, but you are not yet releasing them by shutting the light switch off. How the dog responds will reveal their character. Some are just fine with 10 or 20 commands in a row, while others will shut down after only two. Eventually, your dog will hit the top of their ladder, which will reveal their level of obstinacy and indicate how they see you in the pack structure.

At this point, execute one more command to end the routine on a successful note. Release them with an "Okay!", or whatever your release word is, and give them plenty of affection and excitement. Bring the energy level up and engage with them in some play. Remember the number of successful commands they achieved and work them at that level for a while until they become flawless at it. Then increase this number gradually, always keeping in mind not to push them over their threshold. Trust me, your dog will appreciate the consideration and give you more effort in future lessons.

The stacked stress routine is something you can practice each day, gradually building up your dog's tolerance for how many commands they can manage, or how far up the ladder they can go before they hit their limit. It is a method for building awareness, respect, and trust. Remember not to pet your dog in between the commands, as this is a reward, and keep your voice and energy even-keeled as you move between each command and its mark. Only introduce rewarding contact and bring the energy levels up once you have released them.

COMING TO HEEL

Being able to call your dog to your side and have them put their full attention on you is indispensable to keeping them safe in our world of vehicles, people, aggressive dogs, and other dangers. As with everything else in my approach, I think about this particular command from their perspective first and work backward from there. In the wild, there is no such thing as a wild canine calling another wild canine to heel. Instead, each pack member is always keeping the other pack members in their awareness. They are free to roam around, but they will never go far because if the pack providers decide it is time to travel, each of them needs to follow so they are not left behind. There is also safety in numbers—when a pack becomes defensive, they move close to each other to increase their chances of survival. This is an instinct we can use to encourage them to return to you if they perceive any danger.

My goal for the dogs in our human packs is to train them well enough so they can have this same freedom to roam while

293

keeping us in their awareness. To do this means I need to be able to call them to heel and have them listen immediately if we are presented with a potentially dangerous situation. If I am hiking in the woods, I do not want to keep my dog on heel for five hours. That would be a miserable time for them as it would suppress their natural desire to explore. I want them to be able to wander and satisfy their natural instincts, but if I see another hiker on the trail, or my dog catches the scent of a deer, I want to be able to call them to my side and redirect their attention to me for guidance on what to do next. When the distraction is no longer there, I can release them from the heel, and they can go about exploring the trail once again.

If you keep a dog in heel for too long, when you release them they tend to not want to leave your side, but they are not staying out of some kind of loyalty, they are staying because they are confused about what is expected of them. They might even become more anxious with this uncertainty. While you may think it is desirable to have that much control, what I am going for is providing a life for the dog where they can be their natural self, and letting them roam and explore is an important part of that. Remember, you can never change the internal nature of a dog. You can only encourage and direct what is already present, or you can harm it, causing negative reactions due to psychological trauma.

That said, I always advocate following leash laws. If you need to keep your dog on a leash, you can still give them a little room to explore. Let us say you are walking your dog in your neighborhood—you can hold the leash loosely and let them roam, taking in the smells or finding just the right spot to relieve themselves while maintaining a healthy and safe proximity to you. And when you are ready to cross the street, or you are walking by a neighbor's dog who is viciously growling at you from inside their fence, you can call your dog to heel.

When you say, "Heel!", you are telling them that right now you want them close to you and at attention. You are also giving them the message that you are entering a higher-stakes situation and invoking their trust that you have got it covered. You are de-escalating a situation and reinforcing pack structure when you call your dog to heel. Essentially, you are saying, "Ignore the smells, ignore that crazy dog. I have got this." Once you are across the street or past the barking dog, you can release them from the heel command and once again let them "roam" within the proximity of the leash.

Having the correct intention when using a simple training command such as heel is the ultimate way to create a safe environment and maintain success. Using the command in the interest of safety and to help them navigate our world is an example of how training can have a major influence over behavior.

An important side note here about using the leash. During this (or any) command, you should never tighten the leash or use it as a tether. Consider the leash as nothing more than an extension of your hand and use it as if you were applying pressure for gentle reassurance or direction. A dog should only become aware of its presence if you need to "pop" it as in the last step in the three-part natural communication process (expect, warn, and correct) used for developing behavior that we discussed in Chapter 5. It is important during the training process to help a dog learn what is expected of them. When they are experiencing something new, a leash is a useful tool for reinforcing your request by guiding them in the right direction, if needed. When the dog bonds with you and learns how to be efficient at following your directions, the leash may no longer be necessary. Though, of course, you should still use it in situations that require you to comply with local laws.

It is generally accepted, and I find it to be true, that teaching your dog to heel by coming to your left side gives you the most control when hunting, herding, or walking. While having the dog on the left is standard and is what sporting and competitive regulations expect, it is perfectly possible to train them to heel on the right side if necessary—I have seen this work just fine for people who have a permanent injury, are missing limbs, have limited vision, or just have a personal preference for the other side. For the purpose of my instructions here, I will assume we are training a dog to heel on the left, but feel free to swap the instructions to meet your needs. I will also use "north" and "south" for this example to help discern my orientation versus direction and to minimize confusion.

You will note that these instructions are not based on our perspective. As I like to do with everything, I flip things around to see the world through their eyes. In this case, that would mean if I want the dog to come to heel on the left, the dog would keep us on their right at all times. Do they know the difference between right and left? Maybe not in the way we think of it, but they are tremendously intelligent and have a firm grasp on the complex cognitive skill of spatial awareness. You can teach them to orient by asking them to keep you on one side of them at all times when you give them this command.

I start this routine with something I like to call the "set-heel stage." I walk backward and encourage the dog to maintain me on their right, which naturally places them on my right-hand side. To help make this more clear, I will say that you are facing north but walking south, though of course you could be in any orientation on the compass. Be mindful of where you step, as you are walking backward. Hold the leash loosely and pop it gently to the right to encourage them as you go. Take as many steps as necessary, walking slowly while remaining continuously conscious of their emotional state, until they are walking effortlessly with you on their right, on your right-hand side. You are both walking toward the south together, but because you are facing north you are walking backward while they are walking forward. The more common way to train a dog to heel is to have them always on your left, and if you move backward, expect the dog to walk backward with you or turn and reproach to the left. There is nothing wrong with this method and it does work, but I find my method to be a bit more elegant and easier for the dogs to grasp.

As soon as they come to heel, which means their withers (the base of the neck above the shoulders) are aligned to your thigh, pass the leash around your back and begin to walk forward (north). Say, "Heel!" again, and expect them to circle around behind your back and come to heel on your left. You are both facing the same direction (north), and now you are walking forward (toward the north). The whole time, you are asking them to keep you on their right.

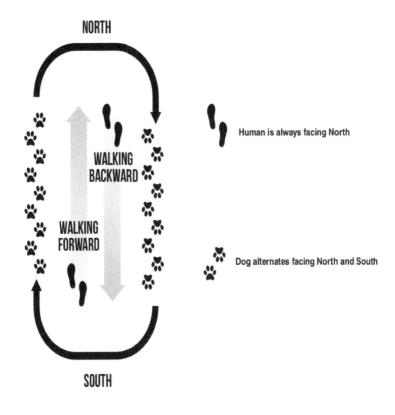

NORTH

Human is always facing North

WALKING
BACKWARD

WALKING
FORWARD

Dog alternates facing North and South

SOUTH

This method of training a dog to heel involves you walking backward and forward while you continue to face the same direction. It trains the dog to always keep you on their right side, no matter which direction you are walking. (Note: "north" and "south" are used to provide context; they are not meant to indicate cardinal directions.)

Continue to walk forward (north) and backward (south),

changing direction but not changing which way you are facing

(you will always walk "north" in this scenario). Each time you change directions, ask them to heel, and they should come around you to keep you on their right. Keep going, switching back and forth, until they get the pattern. In the end, it will be like they are walking circles around you. Once they have a sense of what you are asking, their focus will strengthen and they will naturally tighten up the gap between your thigh and their withers.

As part of the heel routine, you can also condition them to sit when you stop moving. With the dog on your left, holding the leash in your left hand close to their collar, walk forward and use the leash to apply gentle pressure to keep their head and shoulders at your thigh or knee. As you slow to a stop, loosen the leash slightly to give them the opportunity to sit on their own. If they do not sit right away, apply some gentle pressure upward on the leash and give them a moment to sit.

If you have practiced a lot with the stacked stress routine, they may know what you want them to do and respond without you having to say anything. If they do not sit when you give them a second to do so, say the command out loud. When they follow through, encourage them with a calm, low-key, positive verbal marker. Then resume walking and ask them to heel again. Do not release them yet with an "Okay!" or whatever your release word is. Just move forward, expecting them to follow, and then stop again and expect them to sit. The goal is to get them to stay on your left (to have them keep you on their right) when you are walking, and to sit by your side when you stop.

Once they have performed the desired command during the stop and sit phase, mark the behavior one last time, release them with an "Okay!", and reward them with excitement, affection, praise, and play.

Once they have mastered the set-heel stage, they can progress to more advanced levels with almost effortless ease. To make the command more complex, keep introducing variables. Change your speed and change directions. Walk two paces and stop, then walk 15 paces and stop, then one pace and stop. Run sometimes and walk really slowly at other times. Test their external spatial cognizance and hone their peripheral awareness by doing figure eights. Make it random so they get used to staying focused on you and following your lead no matter how stimulating the environmental conditions are. Eventually, you can introduce this command inside of structured play or when you are working on something more advanced, such as developing hunting or herding skills, where you will find this command as useful as on a walk through the neighborhood.

No matter what command you are working with, if at any moment you find that your dog is being resistant to your guidance, stop the training and refer back to Chapters 4 and 5 before you proceed. We want our dogs (and ourselves) to have a positive and fun bonding experience when learning new things. If they understand the structure of the pack, as well as your intentions, they will feel a level of comfort and trust that will result in an eagerness to learn.

THE ROLE OF TECHNOLOGY IN TRAINING

It is clear that traditional ways of working with dogs are effective. After all, they have gotten us to where we are today with our canine companions. It is also clear that there are ways technology can make our lives easier, and sometimes that is useful. When used properly, technology can quickly, safely, and effectively bring our dogs to their full potential. In the past, many of them caused them pain or discomfort—but today there are many that offer positive, safe, and painless ways to work with your dogs. These devices can help you to minimize or even remove hazards, maintain a solid and consistent routine, and get your dog off leash, allowing them room to be themselves. As with anything, however, the magic is not in the tools themselves—it lies in your intention.

GLOBAL POSITIONING SYSTEM (GPS) DEVICES. These gadgets are a real game-changer for training dogs for hunting or search and rescue, or if you are working with a dog who tends to run away when you take them off leash. Taking a dog "off leash" is always risky and unpredictable, especially when you are beginning training. Even well-trained dogs can get spooked occasionally and run off. But for a dog's quality of life, we want them to be able to be off leash, and this tool will give you some peace of mind when you give them that freedom. More advanced GPS units can even provide information about your dog's activity levels and offer extremely valuable insights to help tighten up your training routines.

A GPS collar is essentially a tracking unit that allows you to follow where the dog goes on a handset, computer, smartphone, or tablet. It is a tremendous relief to be able to know where your dog is at any given moment. If I am out hunting and my dog suddenly stops moving, I know where to find them so I can discover whether they have found a bird and are on point or if they have been injured. But remember that no technology is infallible—be sure you have done some preliminary training with your dog and have safeguards in place when you remove the leash and begin to use a GPS system. It is a great complement to training but should never be relied upon 100%.

E-COLLARS. Short for electronic collar, e-collars consist of a collar with contact probes that deliver an electrical current and a handheld device that a person uses to activate the collar. These devices are like virtual leashes, giving you the opportunity to work with your dog at a greater distance than a physical leash allows. They also allow your dog to navigate in places where vegetation may be thick and a leash might get tangled, rendering the dog unable to move in an area that you cannot access. For example, if you are training them to hunt and they run headlong into a thicket, a leash would get tangled and potentially be quite dangerous. E-collars can also allow you more opportunities for training around the home. If you hear your dog rifling through the trash in the kitchen, grabbing your e-collar remote will allow you to work with the dog immediately, without interrupting the event by taking the time to get a leash on them.

Technology for e-collars has come a long way. These devices used to be called "shock collars" back in the day because they delivered a shocking "zap" in an instant. This "dirty stimulus" was designed to use pain as a method of control or punishment through the rapid introduction of electricity—like sticking a fork in a socket. I am completely against this type of treatment, and some of these collars are still available today, so make sure to avoid them.

Instead, search for the more advanced e-collar units that use what I call "clean stimulus," or the gradual introduction of low voltage electricity that slowly enters the muscle, causing it to contract. It is similar to the sensation created by the electrical stimulation that many people receive at the chiropractor or at physical therapy. These devices offer a huge range in stimulation intensity, allowing you to find your dog's comfort zone without the fear of pain. With the evolution of the technology to make it gentler, these new e-collars are much closer to mimicking the natural pressure a dog would feel from momma, like a tap on the shoulder or a "pop" of the leash. As with any device, e-collars can be used improperly, out of ignorance or ill intent, which can cause physical harm or psychological trauma, so be sure to get some professional training that aligns with a positive philosophy in how to use them properly before actually using the device on your dog.

The trick to conditioning an e-collar is positive repetition in a low-energy, learning-conducive environment. You want to get the dog so familiar with hearing your voice in conjunction with the tap on their neck area, by training them hundreds of times, that their conditioned behavior to respond to you is established on a subconscious level. When you "pop" this virtual leash in a moment where you really need them to pay attention—like when they have spotted a coyote and are poised to run—you want them to simply shift their attention back to you and follow your instructions. But you really need to practice the behavior many times before you are in a high-stakes situation. Even then, there are times that their adrenaline will be surging through their body, and the base-level stimulus may go unnoticed. Some units have a dedicated setting (sometimes called a "boost") that gives an increased level of stimulation to help match their adrenal release. If these units are calibrated properly, the dog will receive the stimulation as encouraging, not corrective. However, no device or human judgement is infallible, and success will depend on how synchronized you are with your dog.

It is especially important when working with e-collars to keep the dog's perspective in mind. Remember, all you are ever trying to do is gently apply pressure, much like they would receive from their mamma in the wild. Using high-level stimulus to intimidate a dog into submission is inappropriate and has no place in a healthy relationship.

ELECTRIC FENCES. Traditional electric fences consist of two parts: a wire that is buried around the perimeter of a yard and a corresponding collar on the dog. Some newer versions are wireless and utilize a global positioning system (GPS) or radio-frequency identification (RFID) to establish the boundaries of the fence. These systems are known as geofencing. With both wireless and wired versions, the collar delivers an electrical shock if it gets too close to the perimeter. The collars beep first, giving the dog a warning that a shock is coming. Much like e-collars, some electric fence companies have improved over the years. The old version would shock the dog as they got closer to the fence, no matter which side of the fence they were on. So, if something were frightening or tempting enough to break through the barrier, if they tried to come back home, they would also be shocked. More sophisticated systems will now let the dog back into the yard without a beep or a correction.

But while there are improvements, I am not a fan of most electric fences because they still deliver a sudden jolt of electricity that I refer to as a "dirty stimulus." The dog does not understand what is happening—they just know that when they go into an area, an unseen entity is hurting them, so they simply avoid the area altogether. Electric fences control dogs using fear, but fear is not an effective way to develop healthy behavior. In fact, I have seen a number of cases where dogs become so afraid of the yard and its unseen disciplinarian, they are petrified to leave the house.

I also find electric fences can be the cause of obstinance in a dog or exacerbate structural issues in the family pack. I would venture to say that 50-70% of the families I work with that have problems with their dog's behavior have an electric fence. It is important to the pack structure that you maintain your role as the provider. You want your dog to look to you for guidance, safety, and comfort. When you let them outside to roam by themselves, unattended, you essentially have no guiding influence over them, and you relinquish your role as pack provider. They become masters of their kingdom. They mark their territory, they warn people off, they chase squirrels and rabbits, they dig holes—they are free to do whatever their wild heart desires. Then they come indoors and continue to ignore you and your requests because the pack structure has not been properly established.

I understand the impulse to want your dog to be able to roam and play freely, and if a dog is properly bonded to their pack, this is completely possible without any fencing, electric or otherwise. Fence or no fence, I always recommend you do not let your dog be out in the yard unattended. While it makes sense to want to let them exercise and enjoy themselves, it does not make sense if your ultimate goal is a happy, well-balanced family life. My suggestion to clients with behavior issues that I suspect are related to this dynamic is to be involved in the dog's outdoor activities. Play with them or do a simple walking routine with them three times a day. Be outside when they are free, even if you are up on the porch and they are in the yard. I would venture to say that a majority of dominant, structural-related issues can be resolved with this approach.

FINDING A TRAINER

While I have done my best to provide some basic training routines and shed some light on the fundamental principles of canine behavior, I can only begin to scratch the surface in these pages. While you can absolutely make headway on your own, I strongly recommend you work with a professional to get the best results for your situation. Finding someone with knowledge and experience can save you a lot of trouble and make it easier on you, your dog, and your whole family.

The first thing to understand is the difference between trainers and animal behaviorists. You should have a good sense of the characteristics of these different roles if you have read the last two chapters. Trainers work to get your dog to follow certain commands. They can also train a dog to do tasks like hunt, herd, rescue, or protect. Animal behaviorists are educated in how particular animals act in the wild. This understanding helps them know how to address behavioral issues that are based on the underlying principles of healthy psychology. Some animal behaviorists are trainers (I use training methods to affect behavior and I also train dogs to hunt), but not all trainers are animal behaviorists. If you have significant issues with your dog, look for someone who can do both.

Next, you will want to find a trainer whose methods and philosophy you agree with. The field is full of good trainers who take different approaches toward how they work with dogs. While I do not agree with some of them, there are others who I support even though their methods differ from mine. I will sometimes turn down a client and refer them to someone else if I think our goals are not aligned.

I am interested in helping dogs live out their natural intentions to create happy, healthy, and fulfilled lives. I achieve this through the development of communication that creates solid relationships and harmony in your pack. This is not a quick process. Psychology is not linear. There is no way to know how quickly a dog will let go of fear, settle emotions, or submit to a changing hierarchy. Inevitably, these changes and decisions must be made by your dog, and when that happens is dependent on an infinite number of unpredictable variables. We cannot go to a psychologist and ask for our depression to be fixed by next Friday.

Relationship building takes time. If you are not interested in doing the work to build rapport and bond with your dog, and you just want me to wave a magic wand to get your dog to stop peeing in the house, we are not a good match. But there is a behaviorist or trainer out there that will connect with you and may be able to provide you with what you are seeking. My advice is to interview several behaviorists or trainers. If you get that gut feeling that a method or personality feels off to you, then look elsewhere. Finding the right person can take some time, but it will be worth it in the long run.

When you find someone you are interested in, have a phone call with them and check their references and online reviews. Any reputable trainer or behaviorist will have references you can contact. If you see any reviews online that raise questions for you, ask them. If they get defensive and cannot explain themselves, you may want to keep looking. Keep in mind that not all reviews will be accurate. Some people will post negative reviews based on failures that may be a result of their own abdication of responsibility or lack of effort, not the behaviorists' or trainers'. Be discerning.

Once you find someone you resonate with and decide to work with them, set your preconceived solutions aside and trust them. This might seem like a no-brainer but trusting them means letting go of any better ideas you might have after doing research online, reading books, or talking with friends, other trainers, or your veterinarian. There is a lot of information out there, but when you decide to work with a professional, you are agreeing to accept their expertise and guidance. Do not argue with them or push your own ideas on them. Most techniques and methods have similarities on the surface but achieve different outcomes due to variations in application. Every dog is different, every environment is different, and every person is different. Be willing to follow their lead, and you will be surprised how much change happens.

If you feel uncomfortable at any point, do not be afraid to speak your mind and follow your gut. Any true professional will strive to meet your needs or counsel you in a different direction, if necessary. If you are met with an unwilling, uncaring, unprofessional attitude, then the answers you seek to achieve your goals may reside elsewhere.

There are, unfortunately, some bad actors out there. My advice to you is to do what feels right in your heart and do not accept things at face value. Envision yourself in your dogs' position and ask yourself, "Does this method feel appropriate? Is this acceptable, productive, and aligned with our goals?" Then imagine using this method on your own children. If your answer is "No way! I would never allow this to happen to myself or my children," then do not allow this to happen to your dog and continue your search for a holistic professional. That sentiment betrays my philosophy that your dog is part of your family and should be treated as such. If you do not share that philosophy, you may not share my opinion. Regardless of where you draw the line, if someone crosses it, feel free to call them out or to move on. Neither you nor your dog should take abuse or mistreatment from anyone claiming to be a professional. It is counterproductive and unethical.

You may also choose to work with a team of professionals to help you achieve your goals. Most professional behavior specialists, trainers, and veterinarians want to help your pack find harmony. There is often a spirit of competitiveness and negativity between these groups, but I refuse to participate in such a toxic mentality. We all bring something different to the table, and for those of us who truly have the best outcome in mind for our furry friends, we can appreciate those different approaches. I often get contacted by trainers or clients who have hit a brick wall. I will work with the trainer and the family to find solutions to move past the block so the trainer can resume their progress. I have always loved these scenarios, not only because we all learn something new, and we get the dog one step closer to living their full potential, but because we gain a renewed sense of faith in humanity. Within this meeting of the minds, we experience exponential personal growth as we open ourselves to the beautiful essence of this world. If you speak with a trainer, behaviorist, or veterinarian who badmouths or slanders their colleagues, I suggest you look for someone else to work with, because a closed mind is the equivalent of a rectangular wheel: completely useless.

WORKING WITH A TRAINER ONLINE

You may wonder about working with a behaviorist or trainer online. Do not shy away from it. You may think you need to work in person to achieve your goals, but sometimes introducing a new person into the mix changes how everyone acts, including the dog. Most behavioral misunderstandings revolve around your personal relationship with your dog. Working in a virtual manner removes the influence of the behaviorist or trainer and allows us to address the true nature of the issues at hand: the dynamics that create a healthy relationship.

Working online has not only allowed me to observe relationship dynamics without inadvertently influencing situations, but it also puts the responsibility of working with the dog firmly where it belongs: with the family. I can work with any dog, but that does not necessarily affect the dog's relationship with their family. Working online has required my clients to step up and take their place as pack providers.

I began working with behavior and basic training online part-time in 2019, and after it proved so successful, I shifted almost exclusively to working online in 2020, though there are still scenarios that require my physical presence for more sophisticated training, like hunting, protection, outdoor recreational sports, and service-based tasks. Modern day technology may have its pros and cons, but in this scenario, it allows me to help people geographically much further away than

I could travel. Through the marvel of virtual consultations, I have

the pleasure of assisting people and dogs from all over the globe

to find peace and harmony within their pack.

"When you understand, appreciate, encourage, and manage your dog's nature appropriately, you create a rewarding, safe, happy, healthy, and loving life for them where they can live out their potential as part of your pack."
—David J. Kurlander

7

Getting to the Root of Common Problems

As an animal behavior specialist, I often do not hear from people unless there is a problem. The first thing I do when I speak with someone is assure them that no one is to blame. It is not their fault; it is not the dog's fault; and it is not their last dog trainer's fault. I am not interested in placing blame because it does not take us any closer to solving the issue. Instead, I explain that each situation is unique and consists of a constellation of factors—including the dog's genetic inheritance and early life experiences, the current environment, the physical health of the dog, the person's understanding of dog psychology, and more. We have to approach the situation like it is a mystery to solve, and the best way to understand how to do that is to use the following illustration.

The behavior issues you are experiencing are like the leaves on a tree. They are the culmination of a series of events and circumstances that came before. Any one behavior on the branches—barking, jumping, peeing in the house, etc.—may have any number of causes, which means there is no one solution. We must follow the outer branches back to the trunk and see where they lead us with each individual dog to figure out what to do.

Each leaf leads back to a branch that sprouts from the trunk. The trunk represents the emotional disposition of the dog. It relays information from the roots to the branches, carrying the message with a particular resonance. Is the bark friendly or aggressive? Is the growl an attempt to intimidate or communicate? Are they peeing out of fear or confusion? It is critical to identify a dog's emotional state clearly as the first step in trying to discover the source of a problem.

From the trunk, we trace the emotions back to the roots, which represent the dog's genetics and personality. This is the core of who they are; it is where their fundamental nature resides. As we discussed in Chapter 3, every dog is born with particular attributes, just like humans. They may be enthusiastic or reserved, high-drive or low-drive, strong or not-so-strong alpha mentality, serious or goofy, etc. Some of this can be directed and shaped, but we cannot fundamentally change who they are, and it is important to know and honor the individuality of each dog in sleuthing out their behaviors.

The primary place we can influence a dog's emotional state—which is what we need to do to change the behaviors at the branches—is by paying attention to the soil in which their growth is being nurtured. That soil represents the fundamental building blocks of your pack: structure and communication. Most problems can be boiled down to issues with one, or both, of these, and by tending to the soil on this level—fertilizing it with your time, attention, and effort; watering it with your love and understanding—you will change the emotional output and, as a result, change the behavior at the branches.

There is one more area where you have significant influence, and that is the environment. Wind, rain, sunlight, insects—these all affect how a tree grows and can be a positive or a negative influence. In the same way, creating a safe, comfortable, and happy home can make a huge difference in a dog's emotional state—and thus their behavior.

The Tree of Behaviors

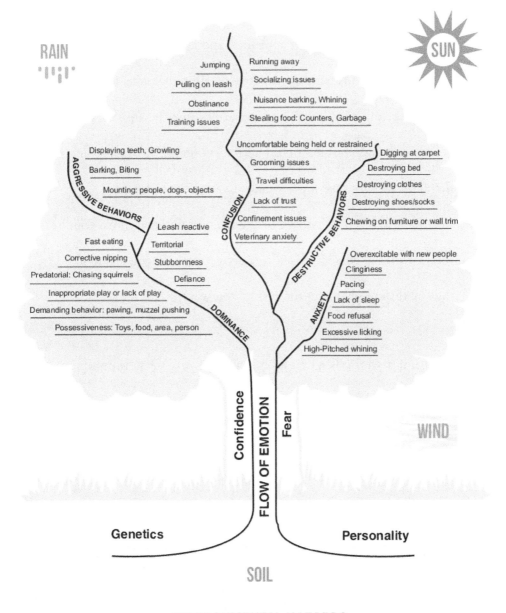

As you can see, much like each tree, every dog is unique, and there are a lot of factors that contribute to their behavior. Do not be overwhelmed by the complexity of the situation. No matter how difficult your problem appears, I encourage you to find the simplicity in it. It is tempting to create elaborate stories to explain their behavior or justify your actions, but often the answer will emerge if you do not let the situation become more of an issue than it is. Do not take it personally. Do not overreact or overthink it. Keep this image of the tree in mind and move your focus from the behavior itself to discovering how you can tend the soil differently to get the results you want.

FIVE QUESTIONS TO ANSWER BEFORE YOU WORK WITH YOUR DOG

Have you ruled out physical/health issues? If you are experiencing a sudden onset of issues with your dog, I recommend you get a full evaluation from your veterinarian. Dogs are stoic creatures, and since they cannot communicate with us using a verbalized form of language, they may develop a behavior that we may categorize as problematic to express they are in pain or experiencing discomfort. I have seen a number of problems disappear completely, from biting to growling to peeing in the house, once the physical issue was resolved. Knowing this information upfront can save you a lot of time and energy that would be wasted trying to fix a behavior problem that does not really exist. Once you have ruled out any physical causes, then you can dive into the rest of the questions.

What are your dog's issues? To discover the source of your dog's issues, begin at the branches, but do not stay there. Trace the situation back through the emotions of the trunk into the roots and look at the soil and the environment too. This exploration requires you to do something I have talked about throughout this book: change your perspective. Saying, "My dog barks too much" is not the dog's issue, it is your issue with the dog. Flip the script and see if you can understand what would cause the dog to bark so much. What are they trying to communicate to you? Why are they acting this way, and what adds fuel to this fire?

Sometimes just shifting your attitude to a spirit of inquiry will loosen something up. If you become aware that your "stubborn" dog is actually an extremely intelligent being with a high work drive, you can start to give them ways to satisfy that streak and contribute to the pack. By appreciating who they are and giving them a sense of purpose, many behavior issues will fade away, and your bond will become closer than ever.

What are your expectations? What do you expect from your dog and what does your dog expect of you? These expectations have to be in harmony. You cannot just take and expect to give nothing in return. This is not how a relationship works. Be clear about what you want from them, and then be honest about whether they can do that for you or not. Likewise, be clear about what you can offer them, based on what they need, and be honest about whether you can provide that for them or not. I am not saying you will need to rehome your dog, but I am saying you may need to think creatively about how you can get support if you need it.

Which method or philosophy are you going to follow? There are many different approaches to working with your dog. Choose one, get all the people in your pack to agree to using that method, and then stick with it. Different approaches are founded on different philosophies, and if you switch from one to another, or you use elements of one combined with another, you will only confuse your dog and have a much harder time creating a harmonious pack. As I tried to make it clear in the previous two chapters, I do not "train" dogs in the classical sense. And to the extent that I use the training tool of command, mark, and release, it is purely in service of addressing behavior issues. That does not mean training is bad. My point here is that the path to success requires you to develop consistency, pick the road that meets your comfort zone, and then stay in your lane.

Is your head in a good space? This is where the power of your thoughts come into play. You must believe in the possibility of change. See your goal and act as if you will reach it. Have confidence in yourself and your dog. Your dog will know and feel when you are about to give up, and they will also feel when you have faith in them and will respond accordingly. Make sure you are resolved and ready to do the work, as sometimes the change will happen quickly, while other times it will be circuitous and require your ongoing commitment. Psychology is not linear—some individuals take longer than others to come around. You may feel like you take one step backward sometimes, but perhaps that is necessary before they can take the next step forward.

Often when you begin to challenge a dog that has gone unchallenged, things can get worse before they get better. Whenever you open the door to an individual's deep psyche and try to understand their motivations (whether human or dog), you do not know what you will find hidden behind the door. You may reveal complicating factors you had no idea even existed but that are strongly influencing the situation. Have patience, remain consistent, and meet your dog's stubbornness with a benevolent persistence. Your attitude feeds the soil and creates the environment that will eventually result in different, healthier leaves (behaviors) sprouting from the branches of your tree, so stay positive and believe!

ADDRESSING COMMON ISSUES

Most of the issues you experience will come down to imbalances in pack/family structure or poor communication that delivers mixed messages and results in confusion. And while I said a moment ago the way through your problem is usually simpler than you think it is, there are also a great many variables at play, given we are dealing with unique animal beings making their home in unique situations, often with several people. My approach does not present a one-size-fits-all philosophy, as I believe there is no such a thing in the complex world of subjective perception, and as such, some might find this section of the book less than satisfying, as I do not offer prescriptions or specific routines for dealing with common problems. Instead, with the image of the tree in mind, I point to places you can look to start to understand your furry family member better. Most of the issues will come down to structure and communication, but your solution will be particular to the individual dog in your life and to your individual circumstances. I encourage you to work with an animal behavior specialist to help you find your way. Often just a consultation or two can give you the right insight or information you need, as well as the confidence to get started.

Barking

Issues with barking, one of the many leaves on our tree, are almost always structural. If you trace the message back to the first branch, perhaps the barking is part of an inappropriate play or maybe it is an act of protection. To begin to investigate the dog's motivation and to get closer to the root of the problem, it is important to discover the emotion behind the barking. Can you hear what message the dog is trying to convey? Let us use an example of your dog barking when someone comes to the door. Feel the energy of your dog. Does it sound like they are saying, "Attention, pack! There is someone here to see us!"? If so, then your dog may be communicating excitement and wish for you to open the door and greet the guests or they may be notifying you with a concern. In this case, they are offering their services to the pack to alert everyone that an outsider is nearby. If they are just alerting you, when you arrive at the door they will step aside to let you assume control of the situation and allow you to determine if it is safe or not.

But if the energy is directed outwardly, toward the person on the other side of the door, they are most likely saying, "Hey! This is MY home! You are not part of this pack and are not welcome here!" This could happen if they have a natural desire to lead. They will step in and do what comes naturally: defend the territory. Or it could be motivated by fear born out of confusion about who is in charge. If they do not feel you can handle the current situation, they may try to take control just to be safe. In either event, you will need to work on establishing your role as provider through routines that build confidence in the structure of the pack. If they accept you as provider but are simply confused, you can emphasize communicating with them more clearly. Identifying the emotion (the trunk of the tree) will be critical to helping you solve the problem.

If a dog has a particularly dominant, alpha-type personality, their barking may rapidly advance into a fight with the other dogs in the home if the other dogs also approach the door or even show any form of communication other than fleeing. In a split second, they will shift their attention from the perceived threat on the other side of the door to a dramatic battle of dominance and begin to fight with their fellow pack mates to demonstrate to them who the leader of the pack is. This is known as redirected aggression. They are saying, "How dare you! I am in charge here, this is my territory, and I have this! Get out of my way and know your place!" So, while the issue might look like your dogs like to fight with no apparent justification, the problem rests with the dog who is being aggressive. Working with that dog to establish structure will typically help realign the pack.

Please keep in mind that working with dogs with dominant personalities or strong leadership tendencies needs to be approached cautiously. If you have a dominant dog with a high alpha-type mentality, they may begin to redirect aggression toward you as you begin to communicate and assert your leadership role. Or they may appear to give way to you while simultaneously establishing their role as second-in-command and continue to use the same amount of force with other pack members. Working with dogs with these personalities will require extra care.

Running Away

Since home is where the heart is, a bonded dog will never voluntarily leave its pack. But if you have a tenuous connection to your pup, and you have a high-drive individual, the predatory instinct will constantly resonate in them and their instinctual response may be to bolt after a squirrel, a deer, or even a car without hesitation. The best remedy is to work on pack structure. You want your dog to look to you for guidance all the time, but especially when they catch a scent or sight prey. The trick is not to redirect their focus or to harm the dog's natural desires, but to encourage them to partake in the natural way they hunt, as a pack, and that means they engage or disengage together. A lot of trainers will try to work with recall, commonly known as the "come" command, but I do not find this effective, especially if there is not a strong enough bond between you and the dog. They may follow this command in lower priority situations, but the moment their instincts kick in, they will make decisions on their own, without your consideration, if the structure is not firm and you do not hold authority over your pack.

Sometimes a dog will run away out of fear. This flight behavior will often happen with newly adopted dogs who have not yet realized they are now part of a pack or who have suffered abuse or trauma that they have not yet moved past. In the wild, when a canine is frightened, they will quickly run back to their pack for support and protection. Running off alone would isolate them and leave them vulnerable, and a "lone wolf" will not usually thrive in the wild. Strength is found together, as a pack, so work on integrating your new family by making it clear that you provide food and safety. Feed them regularly. Pay attention to them. Dedicate some time to shoring up your connection.

One of the more frustrating things for people is when their dog runs away from them but does not go far. Often, they let you get close only to suddenly dart away right when you reach out for them. This uncertainty could be because they are unclear about your expectations, and your forward motion or over focus on them will surely make them nervous. Or it could be that they think you are playing a game of chase according to their rules, and the more frustrated you get, the more fun it is for them. In both cases, the dog is confused about your expectations. This is not so much a question of structure—the dog is not trying to run away from the pack—it is a question of communication. Show them how to play on your terms and let them know what is acceptable and what is not.

Jumping

Dogs jump on people for a number of reasons, so before you decide how to work with your dog on this issue, you will need to determine what the emotion or energy is behind their jumping—which leaf on which branch describes your dog's situation. One option is that they are simply excited to see you. I encourage my dogs' excitement when I arrive home from a busy day. Their enthusiasm transports me from a stressful, demanding day to a space of happiness which invigorates my soul. I wholly accept their blunt force as I tussle with them on the floor. But I am the only one in the family that accepts or desires this behavior from them. They are not allowed to jump on my wife, my children, or guests, and I have communicated that clearly to them. Whatever the rule is that you make for your home, be sure to be consistent with it. You should clearly communicate to them when enough is enough, being explicit about the limits, but most importantly, do not let them jump on you one day and then reprimand them the next day for the same behavior. This will only generate confusion and fear as they do not know how to discern the difference.

Sometimes a dog will jump as a sign of dominance. This will happen if the structure is unclear to the dog and they assume they are in charge. A dog with this motivation feels they need to put you in your place, so they sniff you and overwhelm you with their presence. You may also witness this behavior if there is more than one dog in the pack. The removal of one pack member to perhaps visit the vet or the groomer may trigger a restructuring upon their arrival home. The dominant dog feels like they must put the other pups back in their place. These behaviors may manifest as a mildly overwhelming annoyance to the other pack member(s) or could erupt in a dramatic structural scuffle. Depending on the severity of the situation, you may want to put some effort into your relationship and set the structure with the particular dog that is asserting this form of dominance.

A dog might also jump as a way of playing. If they are nipping at your arms or legs when they jump on you, play is a good guess, and they are simply confused about how to do it. Jumping and gentle biting is how they would play with each other in the wild, and they need to be taught how to play with humans. Be deliberate about communicating to them what is acceptable and what is not.

Some dogs will get overwhelmed with anxiety when their person returns home. I have seen dogs get so excited they urinate or even vomit. This is also a structural issue, but the dog's primary emotion is fear. In the wild, dogs do not leave each other. They are always within earshot of at least some members of the pack, and they regularly do a "roll call" through howling to maintain their connection. If your dog is fearful, and you disappear, they have no way of knowing whether you will be back. It is wholly possible that they experience your departure almost like a death. I have witnessed dogs refusing to eat or drink water for the duration of their person's absence, slowly slipping into a deeply depressive state of existence. I have also witnessed dogs do the opposite behavior, becoming manic and attempting to dig their way out of the home in a desperate effort to find their "missing" pack member.

There is a concept in human psychology called ambiguous loss, which refers to when you lose someone but there is no body. It happens in the case of war or kidnapping, and the survivors are often unable to experience closure. If your dog thinks you are gone for good, but then you show up, imagine the surge of emotions! This level of overwhelm and anxiety is something I often see with clients who have erratic or variable schedules, like nurses, musicians, doctors, police, teachers, and pilots—anyone who might leave the house for seven days and then be home for seven days; who might work 12-hour shifts with occasional overtime on different days every week; or who is home for several months and then returns to a nine-to-five job.

Dogs are creatures of habit and absolutely love routine. If you have a fearful dog combined with a lack of routine, you may have a pup who will struggle with your disappearance and jump all over you with extreme emotion when you return, as if from an untimely departure. If this is your situation, and your dog is experiencing this surge of emotions, be sure not to correct this behavior outwardly with punishment or displeasure, as these may be considered situationally isolated responses. Begin by looking for ways to find consistency within your day-to-day routine. Even if this means finding a dog walker or sitter for those times you are unavailable. However, you decide to organize your days, be sure to do everything you can to stick to it. Remember, dogs will always find safety in "the known."

Biting

Biting is a natural form of communication for canines. Their mouth is as important to them as our hands are to us. They use their mouths to communicate with each other through sounds, grooming, nipping, biting, and play-fighting.

For the most part, puppies do not bite and nip because they are aggressive. They do it because that is what dogs do—it is their way of telling you they want to play. It is our job to communicate to them what is acceptable and what is not, but how you deliver that message is extremely important. If you respond to your puppy's nipping and biting with force, then you will create distance in your relationship and potentially cultivate a dog that is fearful and may someday truly turn around and bite you. If you teach them boundaries when you play, then you will nurture a happy dog and a respectful structure.

To address biting during play, stop your playful participation as soon as they nip you and give a subtle warning by calmly saying "Hey" followed by a gentle "pop" on the leash. You want them to make the connection that it is not the play you are correcting them on, it is the biting. If you stop playing completely when they bite, this will only confuse them and they will bite you again in an effort to engage you in play, like they would with a fellow pack member.

When they have stopped, offer your hand to them again to create a pass or fail situation. Repeat this technique until your puppy gives up their mouthy efforts. Then immediately resume playing at a level of intensity that is acceptable to you. Sometimes offering a toy as a replacement for your hand, such as a knotted rope or ball, can help quell your puppy's natural tactile desire. This would not be considered a reward at this point as you have already expressed clear disapproval for their prior behavior. It would simply serve as a new option for your puppy to solicit play in a more satisfying and natural manner.

When older dogs bite, you have to take time to explore what emotion is flowing through the trunk of their tree. If they tend to bite to get your attention or during play, or when they get excited, their energy will be non-threatening, questioning, or animated. In this case, they may have never learned expectations and boundaries as a puppy. Your dog cannot comprehend the fact that human skin, which is extraordinarily fragile and can be sliced open by something as delicate as a piece of paper, cannot handle their teeth. You can work with them in the same way you would a puppy, communicating to them what is acceptable and what is not.

The emotion behind biting can also be aggressive. If the energy behind their nips and bites feels more corrective or even violent, you may have a structural issue on your hands. Your dog most likely thinks they are the leader of the pack and has the need to keep you in line, so they are using biting to assert their dominance or claim possession over something like a toy or the bed. These bites are often sharp, quick attacks with the intention of putting you in your place. They can be remedied by working on routines to establish structure, but this work needs to be approached with extreme caution. Anticipate setbacks, formulate practical management routines to remove failure to the best of your ability, and always keep in mind the family members or those who may have contact with your dog as they may fall victim to the results of your decisions. Do not let this discourage you—just keep it in your awareness that the path toward love and understanding is not always easy, but it is rewarding.

Another reason a dog might bite is out of fear. I often see this in shelters, an unnatural environment where dogs have little to no experience of stability and must guard what little they have. Upon adoption into and arrival at their new home, a dog may bite out of fear because the bond of the pack has not been formed yet. If you smother them too much before they feel safe and secure, they may respond defensively. I think of this as a natural and healthy fear. They do not know you or the environment yet, and just like when you start a new job or go on a first date, you and your dog are still strangers and must go through a process of developing trust and safety. Let them acclimate and come to you, and when they are ready to emerge from their self-protective shell, they will allow you to make physical contact with them, often through the comfort of play. You will get the best results if you do not attempt too much, too soon.

Growling

Growling is similar to biting—it is one of the primary ways dogs communicate among themselves. And just as with biting, it is important to read the energy behind the growl. Dogs will commonly vocalize when they are in a playful mood—they will grab a toy and shake it, growling with joy. I often encounter the idea that if you let your dog growl when you play with them, you are encouraging aggression. I do not believe this is true. There is a qualitative difference between unhealthy aggression, structural communication, and healthy aggressive play. These are three different emotional states that all may involve growling, but I have seen no evidence that growling during play will make a dog more likely to act aggressively toward the rest of the pack.

If a dog exhibits an increasingly aggressive behavior during a session of play, then what you may have initially thought of as a playful interaction may have been a mild structural struggle between you and your dog that escalated into an outburst of frustration. Similar to how you get frustrated when you ask your dog to do something and they do not do it (like bring the ball back after you throw it), a dog can get angry when things are not going their way.

Because growling is a natural form of communication that is harmless to us, I do not stop my dogs from doing it when they are simply sharing an innocuous opinion or communicating something to me or another family member. I see it as a legitimate way for them to say to my two-year-old, "Enough! Stop trying to ride me like a horse, already!" It is an acceptable way for them to say to other dogs in the pack, "Leave me alone, I am trying to rest." I find this to be a very generous gesture on the dog's part. This behavior indicates a healthy, respectful structure. I would rather they give a warning by growling than escalating the situation with an uncontrolled aggressive outburst. Once they express their displeasure, your role as the provider of the pack is to change the situation. Allowing these communications to go unaddressed may eventually result in an aggressive action.

Discerning when a behavior needs to be corrected or when a dog is communicating in a way that is asking for you to modify the situation to create more comfort and confidence is important. This is why it is important not to assume all growling is aggression. They have a right to set boundaries and set their limits, just as we do.

If the behavior of your dog is not in question, then perhaps there is an issue to be addressed in the larger pack. Are there other pack members, human or canine, who are not respectful? You will need to step in and explain to the human pack members that what one dog (or person) may tolerate, another may not. You may also need to work with other dogs in the pack to help them recognize where the boundaries are with the growling pup. Either way, a solid practical management plan can help guarantee the well-being of all.

While most growling is likely harmless, it is also possible that a dog might growl out of aggression, dominance, or fear. All of these indicate an imbalance in structure and may require different approaches, depending on the cause and the dog's personality. If you are at all nervous to work with your dog around this issue, or you want assistance determining the cause of their behavior, I suggest working with an animal behavior specialist. You will save yourself a lot of time in the long run and you, your dog, and your pack will appreciate the improvements that will likely follow.

Chewing

There is nothing worse than coming home to find your adorable new family member has destroyed the piece of furniture that has been in your family for generations. Unfortunately, dogs do not readily distinguish between an expensive or sentimental piece of wooden furniture in your house and the wooden sticks you throw for them in the yard. Wood is wood to them, and when you get upset at them for gnawing the leg off of your heirloom dining room table, they will likely respond with a look of perplexed confusion. They may also cower in fear, depending on how angry you get, but that does not mean they understand what they did and feel remorse. After all, if they did experience remorsefulness, why would they repeat the behavior again the next time you leave them alone in the room?

There are three reasons dogs typically chew on things.

Possession. If left to their own devices, everything they can reach with their mouth is free for the taking. Your job is to teach them what is theirs versus what is yours. The younger they are when you begin to teach them this lesson, the better. You can teach this lesson using some easy routines that focus on communicating the appropriate structure of the pack. As you make it clear what is yours and what is theirs—and that they do not rule the kingdom—they will quickly adjust to those boundaries and will happily indulge in the sticks and toys they have been given permission to have. You can let them do what they want to those items as long as they are clear that you ultimately possess and provide everything they enjoy. You can achieve this with the use of 'The Choice-Based Behavior Routine' discussed in Chapter 5.

Anxiety. We all get a little nervous sometimes. In response, people bite their nails, twirl their hair, or chew gum. I am a big fan of fidget toys like spinners and putties for times when I have to concentrate on something or do something that does not involve a lot of physical activity. If a dog is anxious or bored, one of the things they may do to help distract themselves is chewing. If your dog is an angel when you are home but destroys the house the moment you leave, you may have an anxious dog on your hands. Some of this can be addressed by creating a clear structure where they feel safe and secure. You can also develop a consistent routine—dogs love predictability and will appreciate knowing when they can expect to do activities with you and when they will be alone.

You may need additional support if your dog is anxious because of abuse or trauma and if you will be out of the house for many hours each day—or if the dog needs to be confined to a crate or a single room for many hours. I am a fan of natural, organic supplements for dogs to help them relax, but only when these products are used in the context of doing everything you can to make your dog feel loved and safe within a pack. Prescription medications can help dogs manage anxiety caused by a chemical imbalance, physical injury, or trauma, but they should only be used for extreme cases and in conjunction with a lot of care and attention.

Supplements and medications are not a replacement for making a sincere effort to work with your dog. If you lead a busy life and do not have enough time to dedicate to your canine companion, then hiring a professional dog service to assist you would be the next best step. If you are not willing to put in the work and spend quality time with your dog when you are home, then perhaps finding a family that has the time and interest would be best for both you and the dog.

Lack of acceptance. Sometimes a dog will just not like another family member or accept their higher position in the pack and will selectively chew and destroy only that family member's things. I have seen this happen within new couples, when the dog has lived exclusively with one of the individuals prior to the formation of the new human relationship. The dog will often accept the other person as an occasional visitor but rebel when they realize that person is now here to stay. I have also seen it happen when a new baby joins the family. The first step toward working with a dog with this mentality is to address the structure of the original pack. Establish that you are the provider, and you possess the territory and everything that exists within it. This tells them that accepting new members and determining new positions within the pack is your job while simultaneously letting them know they are still valuable family members and that these new members are safe and welcome.

If the dog does not respond to this readjustment to their sense of pack, it might mean they just do not like this person. We have all met people we do not like—there is just something about them that bothers us, and we would rather not spend time with them. Sometimes a dog and a person will simply not resonate with each other, much like two positive ends of a magnet that repel each other.

If there is one person in the family who has authority over the dog, it may be possible to get the dog to accept the new person but just ignore them. It can be an uncomfortable detente, like having two children who refuse to speak to each other, or one that pines for the other's attention though they will not give it. It is sometimes doable, but it is not ideal. If you cannot find a workable solution, definitely involve an animal behavior specialist to see if there are other strategies you can try. They can help you assess the situation, including the possibility of rehoming your dog, a tough conversation that may be worth visiting, depending on your circumstance.

Mounting

Mounting, commonly referred to as "humping," has nothing to do with reproduction. When a dog physically restrains another dog and starts thrusting their pelvis, it is typically an expression of dominance through force. If a dog is going to this extent to show they have the upper hand, there is only one option: work with structure. You can try a simple walking routine like the one in Chapter 4. If the dog does not respond to that, you might consider taking them out of their normal environment and working with them in a location where there are a lot of other people, but only if the behavior they are exhibiting is safe and manageable. If you take them to a mall or other location where there are a lot of distractions and they are unsettled and mildly insecure, they have no choice but to look to you and defer to your decisions because you are the only one who will back them up if there is a threat. This form of immersion therapy uses a healthy fear response to help snap them out of their behavior enough for you to begin to work with them on clarifying that you are the provider. Over time, this newly found respect and trust will transfer back home.

Introducing a New Baby

Bringing home a new baby is a big deal for every family member, including the dogs. You can begin the process by making sure that you have solid routines in place with your dog well before you bring the new family member into the mix. Try to base the routines on what you anticipate might be your schedule with the baby, especially if this schedule will differ from your current routine. I know, I know—schedules and babies? I can hear all the parents laughing! There are four children and three dogs in my household, so I know how chaotic it can be. Of course, your routine will require some flexibility, but if you typically take your dog for a long walk in the mornings but do not think you will be able to continue that routine, introduce that change gradually, well before the baby comes home. By setting a structure for walking, feeding, playtime, and personal time that accounts for the newcomer in the family before they arrive, your dog will only be confronted with small changes to their schedule rather than dramatic ones. It will also preemptively deal with any structural difficulties that you might not have been aware were there.

In addition, consider arranging for a dog sitter or dog walker to assist you and your family when you are away from home having the baby, and have them keep as close to your routine as possible. Avoid boarding dogs in a kennel during this time—kennels are fine for vacation, but the disruption may be too much on top of the big change that is about to arrive.

When you bring your baby home, I do not recommend you introduce the baby to your dog right away. Your dog will be excited to see you and will pick up on the high energy level of the family, so their state of arousal will be high. To prevent accidental injury, keep them away from the baby until they have calmed and stabilized, which could take from a few hours to a few days.

When you are ready to introduce the dog to the new baby, take the dog for a long walk, feed them a nice meal, and keep the environment calm. Do not have food or toys nearby—keep the distractions to a minimum. Allow the dogs to come over to the baby one at a time (if you have multiple dogs). Keep the interaction short and sweet. Do not say, "Good boy!" or "Good girl!" in an excited voice—keep the energy in the room low and mellow. Act as if the baby has been there forever and there is nothing to make a fuss about. Remain calm and expect the dogs to follow your lead.

Keep a close eye on your dog's response, remaining aware and respectful of your dog's emotional state. Every dog will respond differently. Some may get possessive and try to aggressively kiss or sniff the baby. Some may not be ready to meet the baby at all and move to get away. Be sure to provide those dogs with the space they desire and offer them a place they can go to be away from the situation if they need more time to adjust.

Remember, as the provider for the pack, you want to communicate that you are the guardian of this baby and that you are taking responsibility for this new family member. Do not allow your dog to participate in the parenting role, even though it may seem cute. This may lead the dog to believe they can correct your child as well. An adult dog correcting a puppy can be helpful; an adult dog correcting your baby can be devastating. If you are nervous about the situation, then it is important to step back and evaluate the reason for your concern. If there is any doubt in your mind that your dog will harm your child in any way, then perhaps pondering other avenues may be required to provide comfort and safety to all. Seek help from an animal behavior specialist to evaluate the situation.

It can take several months for everyone to adjust, so take your time and be diligent. A change in the structure of the pack is a temporary stressor for everyone involved. Everyone in the home will require time to get used to the new family configuration. If you remain confident and calm, maintaining the safety and stability of the pack by ensuring some level of continuity for your canine family members, chances are good they will quickly adapt.

Spatial Possession vs. Territorialism

If your dog growls at you when you ask them to get off the couch, this is known as spatial possession and is a clear indication of an imbalance in structure. If your dog barks menacingly at the delivery truck coming up the driveway, this is known as territorialism and is a communication stemming from a healthy fear of defending their life providing resources from intruders. In both cases, your dog is communicating something about a particular space they are occupying. In the wild, it is important for the safety of the pack to know when someone has come into their territory. So, when your dog barks at a newcomer, this may be a natural response of territorialism. But as we mentioned in the section on barking above, the energy of the bark is important to decipher. If it is indeed aggressive rather than just alerting, you will need to do some structural work to let your dog know that you have the situation under control.

Often, I get complaints about dogs taking over the bed or the couch and not allowing the human members of the family access to these spaces. People often identify this behavior as resource guarding, but in actuality, it is an issue of spatial possession. The dog somehow thinks the bed or the couch is theirs. You will need to work with them to let them know it is yours and you are letting them use it at your pleasure. My dogs are free to be on the couch, but as soon as I walk in the room, they get down. Once I take a seat, they can come back up, uninvited. That may sound a bit weird to some, but it is perfectly natural for dogs. It is similar to when a bride walks down the aisle, or an important speaker approaches the podium. The audience stands up to acknowledge them as a genuine gesture of respect and admiration, not fear. With dogs, there is a pecking order, and they expect to defer to the provider. If your dog does not understand their role, then you will need to work with them based on their personality and on what emotion is driving their behavior.

It is important to note that not all resistance is about aggression or dominance. A dog may growl or give you the side-eye simply to express emotion. Like humans, dogs can get grumpy if someone decides to do something that is against their routine. They may register their discontent with the dog equivalent of a sigh or muttering under their breath, but that does not mean they are questioning your authority and that they want to run the pack (a problem of structure). It also does not mean they are aggressive and are looking for a fight. They may just be defending their own comfort zone or their own personal space. If their sudden outburst dissipates quickly and does not happen again, you can certainly write it off to their mood and learn how to best respect their boundaries. Recognizing that these are individual beings with distinct personalities—and taking the time to get to know them as individuals—will go a long way toward assessing when you have a problem or not.

Housebreaking

The first thing to do if you are having an issue related to your dog going to the bathroom in the house is to have them checked out by a vet. Bladder infections, urinary tract infections, kidney problems and other health issues could be the cause of their mishaps, not bad behavior. Resolving these physical problems might resolve the scenario. If you have ruled out physical causes and the dog is still peeing and pooping where you do not want them to, you will have to put your detective hat on and look at a number of factors to figure out what might be going on.

Housebreaking a puppy is a long process. The general rule of thumb is that dogs do not have the bladder control they need to be fully housebroken until they are around three months of age. I have seen dogs master this big step as young as ten weeks old, but I have also seen dogs take up to six months. Every dog is different, with a different personality and a different background. Your dog may be timid or may not like the outdoors so much, and their personality may affect how quickly they get the hang of relieving themselves outside. In addition, their experience before they arrived at your home might influence their behavior. For example, dogs at shelters often eat, sleep, play, and expel in the same area, and if they formed this habit early on, it could take some effort to reverse this.

If you are dealing with an adult dog who is urinating in the house, and you have ruled out physical health problems, you may be dealing with a dominant or a fearful dog. If they are trickling urine in the same spots in the house at random times during the week, like lifting their leg in high traffic areas such as the corner of the couch or the hallway, they are marking territory. This is a perfectly natural thing dogs do to show dominance and indicate possession of a space, and with some work you can definitely change this behavior. Fearful dogs can be a little more challenging to work with than dominant dogs, but they too can come to feel safe and clear about the structure of the pack over time.

There is no one routine that will work for housebreaking. The trick is to have clear expectations, consistency, and patience. Your expectation should be that the dog will fully expel both urine and feces in a designated area. By keeping to a consistent area, you will minimize their explorative nature so they can maintain focus on the task at hand. Your responsibility is to communicate where that area is to the dog and to offer them opportunities to do this task at consistent intervals. When considering how often to take the dog out, think of the situation from their perspective. How long have they been home alone? How much access to food and water do they have? Is your dog still a very young puppy or a senior dog that may not be able to hold it as long? Take a look at all the variables of your situation and make a strategy.

If you have a dog that is prone to accidents, or one who is peeing out of dominance, you may want to utilize a crate to maintain success during those times you cannot be around. A crate can be a safe and peaceful place for a dog to rest, especially overnight. Some dogs adjust fine to time in a crate, while others may struggle—you will have to observe how your dog responds and work on a positive routine to help reduce stress during the adjustment period.

HOUSEBREAKING SCHEDULE AND CRATE ROUTINE

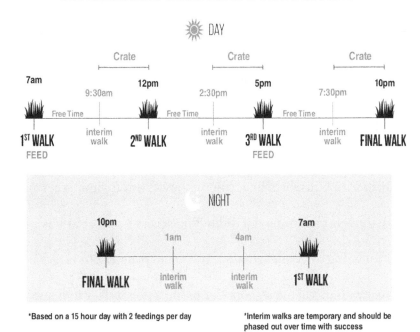

There is no one routine that will work for housebreaking all dogs. This chart offers an example of a routine using a crate and regularly scheduled walks and feeding times. You may wish to modify it to fit your pack's lifestyle.

Dogs are stoic creatures and will typically not show you the extent of their stress visually. What may look mild on the surface, may be extremely severe on the inside. This is why it is important to stay aware of your dog's emotional state. If you see excessive salivation or mild whining, try to limit the initial time in the crate and offer them positive items like toys filled with frozen peanut butter when they do spend time there. Keeping these items exclusive to the crate routine can make acclimation much easier as your dog will start looking forward to these downtime moments.

To help with housebreaking, you may also want to limit access to food, though I am not a fan of limiting access to water as it is too easy for a dog to get dehydrated. If you are planning to be gone for many hours each day, consider hiring a dog walker to come on a scheduled basis. My suggestion is to write down this routine and post it so everyone in the house is on the same page, and then stick to it—consistency is critical to success.

Once your strategy is in place, start working with your dog. When it is time to take them out, put a leash on them and say, "Do you want to go to the bathroom?" Then lead them to the area where it is acceptable for them to go and say, calmly and repeatedly, "Go to the bathroom." If they wish to play or are trying to explore, walk them back and forth in a small line or circle of about five feet, repeating, "Go to the bathroom." Make the whole episode unexciting and boring until they go, at which point you can give them praise and play. Some dogs will be so distracted by exploration and play they will forget to go and then as soon as they get back in the house, they will relieve themselves. If you know your dog has not gone for hours, keep the focus on that before going on a long walk or initiating play.

If you are inclined to take them out for long walks because you enjoy it or you do not have a yard where they can relieve themselves, when you put the leash on, say, "Do you want to go to the bathroom" and take them to a designated area in front of or close to your house and give them time to go. Once they have accomplished this task then you may say, "Do you want to go for a walk?" They will learn the difference. If they go to the bathroom when they are on a walk, that is fine. But you may also want to have consistent times where you take them out for the explicit task of relieving themselves. I require my dogs to fully expel before competitions, work excursions, dog shows, or even before we begin our walks and hikes. Over time this behavior has become automatic for them. This is useful if for some reason you cannot do your walk on a particular day, or you are in a rush to get to work. It will also ensure they do not get into the habit of only relieving themselves on a particular patch of grass that is a mile away from your home.

Once you have started working with your dog, you will need to reach deep inside for patience and fortitude. This can be a long process that requires your commitment. Mistakes will happen, and those are your opportunity to be understanding—your frustration will only delay the process. By remaining consciously aware of your pup and being consistent in your routines, you will eventually achieve a successful outcome.

Fearful Behaviors

Fear has many faces, and more often than not is wildly misunderstood. Not all fear is negative. In fact, when most dogs exhibit fear, it is based on a survival instinct. They may bark at the bicyclist because they see large, fast-moving objects as a threat—which is technically not inaccurate. They may hide when you host a large party, retreating to safety at the back of your closet. Again, not an unreasonable response, especially for the naturally introverted mentality of a canine. Regardless of their motivation, you can encourage them to feel more comfortable or not be aggressive in these situations by removing unreasonable human expectations and respecting their individual needs.

People tend to think fear-based behaviors are the result of abuse, which is less common than you would think. There are, of course, some dogs that have been abused, and they may need extra special attention. To refer back to our tree analogy, these dogs have been trying to grow within a polluted environment in soil that was a toxic sludge. Swap out that sludge for nourishing soil and, over time, with the sunshine of your love and devotion, their emotional wounds will heal, and they will have no choice but to grow and blossom into the beautiful souls they were intended to be.

Regardless of the source, the most common solutions offered for fear-based behaviors are misguided anthropomorphic approaches, such as drugs or coddling. Drugs just suppress the symptoms, do not deal with the underlying cause, and sometimes actually increase anxiety. This can potentially lead to unpredictable and uncharacteristic aggressive outbursts. Coddling or accommodating your dog can also increase their anxiety, which may seem a little counterintuitive. Why would trying to calm them down make them more afraid? Because they need someone strong, clear, and decisive when they are overwhelmed by fear, and if you give them soft, vague, and nebulous, they will be left wondering who will protect both of you. Instead, routines to establish clear structure and clear communication to assure them they are safe will typically yield the best results. Sometimes I will use immersion or exposure therapy, bringing the dog safely into encounters with the thing they are afraid of, but this is not the right approach for all dogs, as this may increase anxiety or cause trauma. A professional animal behavior specialist can help you assess your situation to see if this is a suitable approach.

There are two additional components that are true when working with any behavior issue but that are particularly relevant to fear: time and love. It is natural to want to fix these behaviors as quickly as possible, but time is the essence of healing. The most profound changes will manifest when they are ready and will never appear when you think they should. Rushing these changes will only impede your success. Get to know the unique personality of your canine family member. Maybe they are just timid by nature. If so, honor that by adjusting your expectations. Maybe they do not want to be touched by unknown people or interact with outsiders; that is completely acceptable. Do not force them to be who they are not. Love them for who they are. Offer them understanding and care by making the structure of the pack explicit and communicating to them they are safe.

Not Getting Along with Dogs Outside the Pack

This is a challenging topic that requires us to truly see the world through their eyes. As we explained in Chapter 4, pack is everything. It is where dogs find safety, security, and love. Anything outside the pack is a potential threat to that stable environment. In the wild, canines do not go visit other packs. They do not get together for playdates or to "socialize" in the human sense. Everything happens within the confines of the pack.

Depending on your dog's personality, they may perceive encountering other dogs as a threat, or they may be oblivious to it. They are like children—some kids walk right up to other kids and start playing with little preamble, while other kids hide behind their parent's legs, wanting nothing to do with the strangers you are asking them to go play with. Regardless of each child's personality, when you put them all together on the playground or in a classroom, group dynamics ensue as the kids assess each other. Some step naturally into leadership roles, while others settle comfortably into roles as followers. There are also the rebels and the misfits. As kids encounter the inevitable slings and arrows that come with this process, we explain as best as we can to them about the process of socialization.

Dogs have a similar experience, only with a significant disadvantage: we cannot explain to them what is going on. Some dogs are fine meeting strange, new dogs, while others are not. And when you put a bunch of dogs together, especially in environments like dog parks, the sorting process begins as they look to structure and restructure the pack with every new arrival. With dogs coming and going from hour to hour or day to day, there is rarely an opportunity to form a secure pack. This is why your typically placid dog may behave terribly when put in this situation. Or why a certain group of dogs will play well amongst each other but as soon as one new dog is introduced, they are suddenly all fighting.

A group playdate with dogs outside their pack is an unstable situation that is not suitable for many dogs. It is a hard pill for some people to swallow that dog parks might not be a great setting for their furry family member. Mounting, growling, biting, nipping, and even fighting are common occurrences in dog parks and, if left unattended, a violent fight can eventually be expected. If your dog does not seem to enjoy themselves, comes home agitated, or takes a long time to settle, you may need to take a step back and ask yourself if visiting the dog park is genuinely a good option for them.

Social interactions with other dogs can sometimes exacerbate structural issues at home. If your dog spends time with their own species in a dynamic where they are the most dominating dog, this can boost their ego and reinforce their leadership identity. When they arrive home, they may not be so inclined to let you take over as provider. Dogs who have trust or fear issues stemming from the lack of structure in the home may also receive the wrong message when playing with other dogs. Dogs with this mentality can find solace in the leadership of the more dominant dogs, and if they return back to a leaderless home, they may become more anxious. The solution to this is not to run out and acquire a more dominant dog—instead, you must establish that you are their provider and their source of safety.

Does this mean your dog should never socialize with other dogs? No, it just means there are ways to do it that might be more enjoyable for you and your dog. Have them spend time with another dog they know and see regularly. When you first introduce them, start by taking them both on a walk. When they first meet, communicate to them that you have control over this environment by structuring the walk—have them on a leash and minimize any play. Once they look like they have settled down a bit, let them off leash if you are in a safe location and allow them to have full-contact interaction. The key here is that "you allow them" to interact; you decide when the time is right, and you end it when the time is up. Maintaining the providing role by initially communicating your undeviating dominant position will leave them nothing to fight over. They will find their own dynamic but never question the leadership role that you maintain, essentially minimizing failure within a manageable "play" interaction.

One tremendously important thing to note when letting your dog meet other dogs is to always be aware of your dog's health. If two dogs fight when they meet, it could be as simple as one has an ear infection that has gone unnoticed. Their pain level could cause a violent battle, and if you are not aware of their physical condition, you may blame the fight on aggression or assume these dogs will never get along. This simple practice of mindfulness can easily prevent misunderstanding and injury, or worse.

Not Getting Along with Dogs Inside the Pack

Fighting among dogs in the same household is quite common and figuring out what is going on requires that you look not just at the tree of each individual dog, but also at the entire grove of trees that make up the little forest of your pack. Sometimes you will be able to address an issue with one of your pack members and the problem is solved. With multiple pack members, the dynamic can be quite sophisticated, and you might need to address the issue in multiple ways. Begin by recognizing the personalities of each of your pack members and trying to see the situation from their perspective. What is the emotion behind the fight? Is it fear, uncertainty, disinterest, possessiveness, or something else? If it is one dog's issue, then developing a strategy to work with their emotional state would be a good approach. Keep in mind that what you see on the surface may not be what is actually occurring. Often the one who appears to be the aggressor is actually the victim who is reacting to a silent instigator. Not to start an interspecies war here, but if there is a feline in the house you may want to start there, as they are masters at subtle insult and provocation.

While any two dogs can fight, in my experience, most fighting happens between two female dogs. As I wrote about in Chapter 4, it is my opinion through extensive observation and research that females are in actuality the most powerful members of a pack. The general scientific literature on pack structure does not deem them the official pack provider, but I see them as the keystone member. To raise the next generation, including the future providers, requires incredible strength, intelligence, and finesse. As such, I find female dogs to be generally more tenacious and stubborn. This is, of course, a generality. But by far I see many more fights between female dogs than I do female to male or male to male. Regardless of their sex, if you have two genetically born leaders, you may have your hands full.

The most common reason for dogs to fight is because one or more of them are unclear of your position as the lead provider. If they do not know who the boss is, one of them (or maybe more than one) will try to step in and be the provider. Working on routines around structure and improving your relationship with the pack will clarify this and resolve the problem if that is indeed the cause.

Another reason dogs will fight among themselves is a lack of acceptance. This can happen if you adopt a new dog into an existing pack. As the pack provider, you can make it clear this new member is accepted and protected by you. You can reassure everyone they are safe by making sure everyone knows there is enough food, attention, and love to go around. That may mean giving each dog individual time with you for play and connection as well as activities for the pack as a whole.

"Dominant" / "Stubborn" / "Aggressive"

There is a lot of confusion out there around the type of behavior often described as "aggressive." I find that most of the dogs that get labeled as aggressive are actually dogs who have a natural, healthy, dominant personality with a strong oppositional defiance. Yes, they may act aggressively at times, but they are not unpredictable and dangerous, which is what people are implying when they say their dog is dominant or aggressive.

Before I go on with this, I would be remiss not to include a caveat here. If you are afraid of your dog and/or you do not know how to read their behavior, I encourage you to work with a professional. Do not put yourself or your family members at risk. Do not put the dog at risk. Your fear alone will make it impossible to get good results without assistance. Reach out to a professional animal behavior specialist to help you navigate the situation.

Dogs with a natural spark of leadership, with a dominant personality, are often very stubborn. They may growl at you to communicate their feelings, muscle you or other dogs out of the way, or ignore you when you ask them to do something. If they feel like a petulant teenager, then it is likely you just have a headstrong, willful personality on your hands. These dogs are often very smart—they are born leaders after all—and will need a little extra effort.

Standard routines to develop structure are important but be prepared to have to work extra hard to overcome their stubbornness. I once worked with a one-hundred-and-fifty-pound dog that refused to walk on the leash for his human pack members. To work with him, I did a typical walking routine, but when he laid down and would not go any further, I just kept calmly popping the leash, tapping him on the shoulder as it were. It took nearly forty-five minutes—the longest of any dog I have ever worked with—for him to finally stand up and follow me on the walk. Your stubbornness needs to outlast theirs. You must be a mountain that they cannot move.

Intelligent dogs also want to do interesting things. If you are leaving them at home all day with no activities and have little time to offer them ways to contribute to pack life, they are going to feel unsatisfied, and you may encounter more obstinance from them. Make the time to give them an outlet to satisfy their natural desires through play. Take them places with you, side-by-side, so that they can experience pack roaming as they engage with a wider diversity of experiences that the world has to offer. Be just a little more stubborn than them, and you will find that you truly have an engaging and loving family member.

BE PATIENT!

I hope this chapter gives you a sense of clarity and a mindful way to approach your furry family member with curiosity and interest. As I said at the outset, I do not offer recipes for how to solve common problems because each case of biting, chewing, or barking has a different emotional cause and a different root, and thus will require unique adjustments to the soil, water, and environment, to return to our tree metaphor. This is a vastly different way to relate to your canine companion than what people typically encounter, which is why I spend so much time on your capacity to shift your perspective, tap into the field of potentiality, and find patience, love, and understanding. We are in an emotional and meaningful relationship with these beautiful animal beings that we have chosen to share our lives with. We owe it to them to see them in their fullness and accept them for who they really are. To commit to working with them to achieve a balanced, happy, and harmonious life together is one of the greatest joys you will ever experience.

Discovering one's inner ability to let go of personal thoughts, emotion, culture and prescribed social norms is a feat all in itself. Then to allow your mind to see through the eyes of another is an enlightening and life changing experience. The meaning of mindfulness and our abilities to achieve it beckon to surface.

—David J. Kurlander

8

Depth and Dimension

As you arrive at the end of this book, you are also beginning the first chapter in your own tale with your pup. That story is unique and will unfold in unforeseen ways, especially if you commit yourself to being mindful, patient, and open to what is possible. There are as many ways of knowing and seeing the world as there are organisms on this planet. Open your mind to this fact, and you will be able to have a relationship with your dog that you cannot even imagine from where you sit now.

Sharing a life with a dog is a big responsibility. We have brought these beings into our world and most of them would not survive on their own in the wild. We owe it to them to love them and provide the best life for them that we can. Much like having a child, developing a relationship with a dog can be one of the most rewarding things you will ever experience. But you must approach the relationship with a certain frame of mind, one that honors the individual beings that they are. You must let go of judgment and release any preconceived ideas about humans having dominion over animals. We have a responsibility as custodians, yes, but the master and servant model have no place in a relationship of mutuality.

Dogs have a rich life, one brimming with a full range of emotions and a desire to live out their purpose. How will they do that in our human world? That is up to you. Will you make them conform to your idea of who they should be, or will you listen deeply and help them live out who they really are? If you stop anthropomorphizing them, and cease projecting your ideas onto them, you leave an opening for yourself to get curious about their inner life. Curiosity is key to being able to think outside the box, see things from a different perspective, and tap into the field of potentiality to find unforeseen solutions to perceived problems.

In this book, I have tried to offer you a sense of what it is like to step outside your own reality and into the mind of another. It will take practice. A closed mind is like a thick, opaque wall. You will have to use all the tools at your disposal—mindfulness, meditation, perspective-taking, shamanic practices, external support, and more—to find your way into this new paradigm. You have an incredible opportunity to move beyond simple training tools to reach a higher level of integrity and connection in your relationship with your dog. The world tells us we must feel certain things and behave in particular ways to achieve certain ends, but I do not buy into that notion. Much more is possible for us if we only open to it.

The rewards of being a responsible custodian of the dog you have chosen to share a life with go well beyond just having a well-behaved pup. As you get more practice seeing the world through their eyes, you will begin to expand your senses to include other organisms. You may notice one day that you wonder how the tree outside your front door experiences you when you pass by it on your way to work. Or you might think about the experience of the sunflower as it tracks the sun across the sky. When you begin to shift your awareness like this, you will discover an overwhelming sense of connection and belonging. This recognition of our interdependence is key to the survival of all the species on this planet—from human to canine and beyond.

The precious ecosystem of the Earth provides us with everything we need to live. When we are disconnected from it, we can do things to it that are against our own interests. Right now, we approach our world in the same way we did with old paradigms of dog training: using force and coercion to get what one party wants, often at the expense of everyone else involved. But when you truly get to know another being on their terms, it begins to change things for you. When you love something, you do your best to care for it and help it thrive. If you can do this with your canine companion, I believe there is hope for the planet.

My ideas are not meant to be the last word. In fact, as any good teacher will suggest, I urge you to test them out for yourself. My experiences, theories, and research are but mere stepping stones for further thought and exploration. Use what works and leave what does not. Build on it and refine it for yourself. Then take that learning into the living laboratory of your family pack and begin your unique story. And if you feel moved to, begin to speak for those who cannot speak our language, canine and otherwise. They are counting on us.

Afterword

Dedication, passion, and an internal calling. These are a few words that describe David and how this book has come to be. The manifestation of this book is beyond anything I could have ever imagined. Every story, and every dog in this book, have left an everlasting imprint on our soul. It is never just a training lesson with David; it is so much more. This book is an enlightening journey of love and represents the creation of the profound relationship between humans and canines.

Fate has been writing David's and my story all along. We met under circumstances that deserve a book on its own. We were connected—mind, body, and soul—the instant our eyes met. That moment didn't feel like our beginning, rather, it felt like our reunification. But that's a story for another time.

Upon meeting David, his passion for animals and devotion to his four-legged students was immediately evident, and it was one of the many reasons I fell in love with him. To this day, David's phone never stops ringing. His schedule is booked solid from morning to night, seven days a week, including holidays. I have witnessed him leave the house at two o'clock in the morning and head to a shelter to help a dog. His dedication never ceases to amaze me.

The purpose of this afterword is to give you, the reader, an inside perspective or a "behind the scenes" view into David's life, so you know how the book came about and why it is one of the most important accomplishments of his life. I have personally experienced the profound impact this man can have on a life and a family, and it has changed me in more ways than I can express. Yet David will always humbly remind me that he is merely a conduit of information, and it's the owner's ability and willingness to put in the time and effort that ultimately creates the everlasting bond with their dog.

Most of us only dream of the opportunity to do work in which we are as passionate as David. However, working in this occupation, especially with such devotion, comes with its challenges. Many people can leave a bad day at work behind. However, for David, bad days often involve situations that cannot be unseen or easily forgotten—from witnessing the heart-wrenching aftermath of abuse and neglect to enduring the passing of beloved dogs with which he had the privilege to work—it is not a career for the faint-hearted. Every instance has become a part of David, woven into the very fabric of his soul. The shelter days are the most difficult for him, knowing that he won't be able to rescue every single dog regardless of the many he does help. Nevertheless, he puts his heart on the line and perseveres despite the emotional toll he pays.

I don't blame David for preferring the quiet isolation of the forest and his inclination to study wild canines that are naive to the brutality of mankind; however, he has an undeniable gift for working with aggressive and fearful dogs that have suffered at the hands of abuse. It is a calling that cannot be ignored. Still, the emotional effects of this work are slow to fade, if they do at all. For instance, a plastic bag on the side of the road may appear innocuous to a passerby but is a trigger for David as it may contain the remains of a dog or a litter of starving, suffocating puppies.

On occasion, I have seen wounds inflicted on David when he is working with an especially challenging dog, yet never once have I seen him give up. If anything, this fuels his drive and passion. I marvel at his ability to see beyond negative behavior and find the potential within a dog that just mauled his leg. But I'm not at all surprised to witness that very same dog greet him a few weeks later with excitement and kisses. Whereas most others would give up and recommend euthanasia for these dogs, David sees hope, potential, and a lost soul who simply needs to be heard.

Though the heart-wrenching moments come with overwhelming sorrow, David insists that joyous moments are abundant in his line of work. My favorite part of the day is listening to the heartwarming stories he tells about the progress he has made with his students, the new friends he has met, and the ideas he has devised from gathering new experiences and discoveries out in the field. I've seen firsthand the joy and hope that result from his dedication, which serves as a comfort for us on difficult days.

I have discovered from David (and I hope you have as well) that learning to understand and communicate with your dog is not "training" per se. Rather, it should be viewed as a lifelong journey toward developing a deep connection with your dog. I've been fortunate to have a dog in my life since childhood. However, my newfound knowledge of dog psychology has enlightened me to the profound bond that can form between human and dog. I felt the true depth of this bond when I first met our dog, Riley.

Despite Riley's history of abuse at the cruel hands of others, David found him, lifted him up, and carried him from this dark place so that his soul could rise like the sun bringing on a new day—a day of comfort, love, and safety. It was remarkable that, given Riley's challenging past, he was able to jump over the hurdle of cruelty and give pure love to my family and me. He was my "soul-dog" and inspired me daily. Being able to understand and meet Riley's needs enabled us to form an unbreakable bond. I experienced a level of love from Riley that I never knew existed between human and canine.

David's research and methods challenge the way we view dog psychology and render many old-school humancentric dog training techniques obsolete. The reaction to this new approach has been a mix of admiration and some disagreement. For the most part, many dog trainers and behaviorists who seek a new way of relating to animals will reach out to David to learn more about his methods. David will always commend, appreciate, and admire those who seek to improve their practices; after all, this mentality is how the world will move forward and progress. On the other hand, David's progressive approach has enraged many self-proclaimed trainers (I use the term "trainer" very loosely) as it challenges their cruel and abusive methods. David vehemently condemns the use of abusive devices and techniques, and he has proven to these abusers that he is a force to be reckoned with.

Every dog that David has worked with has had a profound impact on his existence and enriched his heart and soul. He has often expressed that in his profession, no two situations are the same. Though some might share similarities, none are identical, and this is what widens his eyes with wonder and fills his soul with excitement. To live in a world that surprises you every day, full of wonderment and inspiration, is something I believe every human should strive to achieve.

David's passion for his professional work and all living beings is immeasurable, as is his love and devotion to his wife and children. I am proud of all his accomplishments and can't wait to see what more the future holds.

Love,

Tammy D. Kurlander

ABOUT THE AUTHOR

David Joseph Kurlander is a leading voice in the field of animal behavior. As a world-renowned animal behavior expert, domestic and wild animal trainer, and researcher, David is dedicated to understanding how other species perceive life and how humans can better meet their expectations. For over 25 years, David has traveled the globe to help more than 150,000 domestic canines and their families achieve a healthy and harmonious life together.

David's immense love of animals was evident around the age of four when he developed a deep bond with his Siberian husky, Brandy. This strong connection sparked David's interest in animal behavior and ignited a life-long passion for working with various species. As a teenager, he worked in local pet stores and managed breeding programs for reptiles and spiders for private collections. He was a Wild Animal Keeper for the Wildlife Conservation Society in New York City, and has worked with many other well-known organizations, including Rescue Dogs Rock NYC, S.N.O.R.T (Short Noses Only Rescue Team), and Paws Crossed in Elmsford, New York.

David is the founder and owner of Steady Wind, LLC, where he works with canines and their families in implementing proper structure, developing crystal-clear communication, and creating deep trust within the "pack." David's non-aggressive approach and unique ability to understand canine emotion and psychology produces rapid and lasting results. David is also the host of *The Pack Animal Podcast*, where he regularly dives into the inner workings of a dog's mind and behavior and conducts dynamic interviews with a wide array of guests and experts.

He spends his free time with his wife and four children, as well as hunting with his canine companions.

He can be found online at SteadyWindDog.com and ThePackAnimalPodcast.com

In Loving Memory Of

My eternal brothers, companions, teachers, and familiars:

Brandy, Winston, Nanuk, Angus, Cinder, Riley

The love we share transcends death and continues to inspire this lifelong project. Our indestructible bonds have fueled my dedication to helping others to see clearer—with closed eyes and opened minds.

With each coming and passing, you added a piece to my heart and filled my soul with meaning. You are the shining lights that illuminated my path to becoming the person I was always meant to be. For this, I am eternally grateful. You remain by my side through the trials and tribulations of life and your presence has never faded. Together forever is our way, and together forever we will remain. You are the source of my love and inspiration.

We are pack and inseparable, and without you this book would not have come to pass.

To my Ancestors, passed but never gone:

Ethereal whispers gently grace my mind and soul as the winds of fate have transformed me, The Norns have guided me, carrying the echoes of knowledge and wisdom of my ancestors, which resonates within my existence, providing eternal inspiration. Visions of my origins expand beyond boundaries, bringing clarity to reality. To live as we once were, at one with our world, as beings of gratitude and free of corruption from installed false truths.

You have taught me how to breathe life, not air.

Your passing has only brought us closer together. I feel your hands on my shoulder each and every moment, protecting me and guiding my heart. One day I will sit among you and guide my children as you have done for me. My heart is filled with bliss knowing we will be reunited once again.

Your influence and love have not gone unnoticed.

The Magic within spoken words is powerful beyond comprehension. Words are a manifestation of thought, intention, and emotion that can bend the will of a soul, elude the masses, and alter reality itself. With one word, one can provoke pleasure, pain, comfort, fear, love, or hate. Even a single word may contain several responses depending on how it is emotionally expressed.

One solitary word can tell an infinite story.

One single word may start or end wars.

One simple word may dictate the beginning or the end of a life.

—David J. Kurlander

References

Andics, A., Gacsi, M., Farago, T., Kis, A., & Miklosi, A. (2014, February 20). Voice-Sensitive Regions in the Dog and Human Brain Are Revealed by Comparative fMRI. https://pubmed.ncbi.nlm.nih.gov/24560578/

Berkoff, M. (2008). *The Emotional Lives of Animals: A Leading Scientist Explores Animal Joy, Sorrow, and Empathy — and Why They Matter*. New World Library.

Berns, G. S., Brooks, A. M., & Spivak, M. (2014, March 6). Scent of the familiar: An fmri study of canine brain responses to familiar and unfamiliar human and dog odors. *Behavioural Processes*. https://www.sciencedirect.com/science/article/pii/S0376635714000473#:~:text=Importantly%2C%20the%20scent%20of%20the,a%20positive%20association%20with%20it.

Brigham Young University. (2009, July 21). Babies Understand Dogs, Bark-matching Study Finds. *ScienceDaily*. Retrieved July 29, 2021 from www.sciencedaily.com/releases/2009/07/090720163559.htm

Chopra, D. (2011). *The Seven Spiritual Laws of Success: A Practical Guide to the Fulfillment of Your Dreams*. Amber-Allen Publishing.

Coren, S. (2014, April 1). *A designer dog-maker regrets his creation*. Psychology Today.

https://www.psychologytoday.com/us/blog/canine-corner/201404/designer-dog-maker-regrets-his-creation?page=1&eml=.

Darwin, C. (2009). *The Expression of the Emotions in Man and Animals.* Oxford University

Press.

Freud, S. (2009). *Totem and Taboo.* Digireads.com

Goodall, J. (2006, June 24). *Secondary menu.* Transcript: Jane Goodall on Chimpanzee and

Human Emotions | Jun 24, 2006 | TVO.org. https://www.tvo.org/transcript/855384/jane-goodall-on-chimpanzee-and-human-emotions.

Grout, P. (2013). E-Squared: Nine Do-It-Yourself Energy Experiments That Prove Your

Thoughts Create Your Reality. Hay House Insights.

Hollis, J. (2015, July 28). *What is a Projection? Presented by James Hollis, Ph.D.* YouTube.

https://www.youtube.com/watch?v=gL9isdHw9CQ.

Nagasawa, M., Mitsui, S., En, S., & Ohtani, N. (2015, April 1). *Oxytocin-Gaze Positive Loop and the Coevolution of Human-Dog Bonds.* Researchgate. https://www.researchgate.net/publication/275050273_Oxytocin-Gaze_Positive_Loop_and_the_Coevolution_of_Human-Dog_Bonds.

Nicholas, C. E., Wegienka, G. R., Havstad, S. L., Zoratti, E. M., Ownby, D. R., & Johnson, C. C. (2011, July 31). *Dog allergen levels in homes with hypoallergenic compared with nonhypoallergenic dogs.*

American journal of rhinology & allergy.
https://www.ncbi.nlm.nih.gov/pmc/articles/PMC3680143/.

Pennisi, E., Normile, D., Fritts, R., Wadman, M., Pérez Ortega, R., Viveros, A., & Ibrahim, M. (2019, January 9). *Dog breeds really do have distinct personalities-and they're rooted in DNA*. Science. https://www.sciencemag.org/news/2019/01/dog-breeds-really-do-have-distinct-personalities-and-they-re-rooted-dna.

Taylor, Bernie. (2017). *Before Orion: Finding the Face of the Hero*. Aquila Media Group.

Winerman, L. (2005, May 1). *When dogs bark, humans understand*. Monitor on Psychology. https://www.apa.org/monitor/may05/dogs.

Thank you!